I WISH THE RAINBOW
BRIDGE HAD VISITING HOURS

A Veterinarian's Memoir of
Love, Life, and Letting Go

By Dr. Brian E. Joseph

https://www.advantage-publishing.com

ISBNS

Ebook: 978-1-954024-50-2
Paperback: 978-1-954024-51-9
Hard cover: 978-1-954024-52-6

To contact, please e-mail: brianjoseph522@gmail.com

Table of Contents

INTRODUCTION

I recently told my eldest son, Dr. Zachary Joseph, a companion animal veterinarian in the Minnesota Twin Cities area, that at least six books were outlined in my head.

Dr. Zack asked, "Why are you writing books?"

My answer was, "Because I am going to die!"

I didn't imply my death was imminent. Mercifully, we rarely know the exact time when our candle would burn out but mine recently came close in Kurdistan. I did not fear Death's approach, although he is a bit of a bitch because my life has been full and interesting. But it occurred to me during the three hours I was mostly unconscious that if I didn't tell these stories, then the stories would vanish with me.

In 1974, one of my early veterinary mentors, Dr. Chuck Sedgwick, a former veterinarian for NASA, the San Diego Zoo, and the University of California, Davis, School of Veterinary Medicine, said one's goal should be to walk gently through life without leaving a mark. Dr. Sedgwick left a lasting, positive mark on many animals and people (including me), not despite this intention, but more likely because of it.

On the other hand, First Nation people say that no one is really gone until no one speaks their name anymore. I don't care if anyone speaks my name, but I would like them to speak the names of the dogs that made my life richer.

I love dog books, movies, and stories, although they always make me cry. Even cartoon dog movies make me cry. I know this is going to happen before I pick up the book, the magazine, or turn on the movie. It is guaranteed.

If I really think about it, I think I submit myself to reading, watching, and experiencing dog stories because I can't get enough of dogs. I simply can't. They are not fur balls to me; they are fur angels, best friends, and soulmates. But, like the candle that burns brightest, they burn for a short time.

I think back to Shane, a six-year-old South African whose story was reported in the *Global* on June 29, 2018. Belker, the family's then ten-year-old Irish wolfhound, was dying from cancer. Nothing could be done to save him, and the family's veterinarian gently offered to euthanize Belker in their home, sparing Belker a trip to a less comfortable clinic environment. Shane's parents agreed, thinking he might learn from the experience.

Shane petted Belker for the last time as the dog slipped away. Shane was so calm. The veterinarian wondered if the boy truly understood what had happened. The family wondered aloud why dogs have shorter lives.

"I know why. People are born so that they can learn how to live a good life – like loving everybody all the time and being nice. Dogs already know how to do that, so they don't have to stay for as long as we do," Shane said.

See? Now I made you cry. That didn't take long.

As a veterinarian blessed with a diverse career, I have provided painless deaths to many animals: antelope, beluga whales, birds, cats, cattle, dogs, elephant seals, fish, foxes, gorillas, harbor seals, horses, reptiles, sea lions, sea turtles, and almost any kind of animal you can imagine, including two of my own dogs.

It has never been easy, nor should it be so. Each time, I apologized to the animal and said goodbye. Each time, I understood the animal was affected by a terminal condition with no hope of recovery, had a poor quality of life, and suffered. Each time, their death brought tears to my eyes even though I knew I was doing the right thing.

I have a deep reverence for life and deep admiration for companion animal veterinarians, like my son, Dr. Zack. Euthanasia of suffering companion animals is part of his everyday work routine. I recently asked Dr. Zack how he copes. His response was rooted in something he learned in childhood.

"The loss of Pepper (our first Bernese Mountain dog) taught me that death is a part of life. Learning that dogs don't live forever helped me learn to compartmentalize their loss. It makes my job as a veterinarian easier on a day-to-day basis," he said.

I don't know how he does this. I am not that tough. I also have deep reverence for those who handle the remains of companion animals. By my standards, this also is God's work.

Throughout this book, you will meet the members of our pack, including our Bernese Mountain dog, Peppermander, who will argue that she is the GOAT because of how she managed her pack, and she is the reason why we are talking about this at all. In the subsequent book, you will meet Anniecan Mander, Pepper's competitor for GOAT, because of the thousands of hours she contributed to making people's lives better. But this first book is about what led us to Pepper and what she gave us over the course of her life. In the subsequent book, as you journey through more stories, you can decide for yourself who you think takes the crown, Pepper or Annie.

Although this is not her story, Anniecan, known to her friends as Annie, passed away on September 7, 2022. Like all of our dogs, Annie was cremated and like all our dogs (and the cats, if the cats ever die), Annie and the rest of our pack's ashes will be mixed with our ashes when we pass and will be returned to the sea. That responsibility rests on the shoulders of our almost-daughter, Wendy Spaulding, aka Wendell, who you will meet later in this story and come to love as we do. Annie was cremated by Over the Rainbow Bridge in Olalla, Washington. They returned her ashes with this anonymous poem:

Just this side of heaven is a place called "The Rainbow Bridge."
When an animal dies that has been especially close to someone here,
That pet goes to The Rainbow Bridge.
There are meadows and hills for all of
Our Special Friends, so they can run and play together.
There is plenty of food, water, and sunshine,
And our friends are warm and comfortable.

All the animals who had been ill and old
Are restored to health and vigor,
Those who were hurt or maimed are made whole
And strong again, just as we
Remember them in our dreams of days and times gone by.
The animals are happy and content,
Except for one small thing: they each miss
Someone very special to them, who had to be left behind.

They all run and play together,
But the day comes when one suddenly stops and
Looks into the distance. Her bright eyes are intent;
Her eager body quivers.
Suddenly she begins to run from the group,
Flying over the green grass,
Her legs carried her faster and faster.

You have been spotted,
And when you and your special friend finally meet,
You cling together in joyous reunion, never to be parted again.
The happy kisses rain upon your face;
Your hands again caress the beloved head, and
You look once more into the trusting eyes of your pet,
So long gone from your life, but
Never absent from your heart.

Then you cross "The Rainbow Bridge" together...

I am not sharing these stories, these lives, because they are sad, even though parts of their stories are sad. All our canine family members left us too soon, but as it is said, they have all wrapped their paws around our hearts and have all taught us lessons about love and devotion.

I ask you to consider an equation that is the thread running throughout this book. On one side lies the pain we endure when we lose a fur child. On the other side of the equation (think teeter-totter, if they are still a thing and have not been outlawed due to safety concerns), think of the joy they give to us during their brief lives.

After you do the math, I am sure that you, like me, will conclude that we are the winners because we are able to share in their lives. I hope you enjoy reading their stories as much as I have enjoyed being part of them.

As long as someone reads these stories, they won't really be gone.

See, I made you cry again.

This is not intended to be a comprehensive guide to dog breeds. There are many such books. My intention is to provide enough information concerning the breeds discussed here so that those less familiar can develop a feel for the character of a handful of breeds that have been a part of the fabric of my life. Everything contained herein represents my thoughts and the way that I remember things. It is not intended as gospel nor intended to spark contentious discussion concerning dog breeds. They are just my opinions, and I apologize for any imperfections in my recollections.

As a bit of background, depending on your source, somewhere around 400 dog breeds exist today. The American Kennel Club (AKC) recognizes 137 breeds divided into six groups: sporting, hounds, working dogs, terriers (known in our household as terrierizers), toys, non-sporting, and herding dogs. That is a wide spectrum. Wider still when you consider that the smallest adult Yorkshire terrier might weigh as little as four pounds, while an adult great Pyrenees might weigh as much as 150 pounds.

A close and irreverent friend of mine once told me that anything small enough to be carried off by a raptor or to be eaten by a snake is not a dog. That friend had five chihuahuas near the end of his run! My personal preferences have focused mainly on sporting and working dogs. A great book concerning dog breeds and dogs in general is the *UC Davis, School of Veterinary Medicine Book of Dogs: A complete medical reference guide for dogs and puppies,* edited by Mordecai Siegal, HarperCollins New York 1995. The American Kennel Club website also has very useful information concerning dog breeds and dog care.

I am grateful for the many people who shared their memories of our dogs. You will come to know them as the tribe associated with our pack that includes my lovely wife, Sally, who has shared not only our canines but our sometimes up and down journey for almost three decades, along with our two sons, Zachary and Maxwell, our almost-daughter Wendy Spaulding, and her husband Chris Spaulding, our almost son, Gabriel Policani, our close friends: Traci Belting, Hali Eden, Angie Ireland, my darling niece, Dr. Amy Kizer, Paul Povey, Cindy Roberts, Dr. Annie Seefeldt, Dr. Danny Skirvin, Dr. Stan Stearns, the founder of the Gabriel Institute, and Becky Wilson. I also want to thank Denise Dean, a.k.a. Grandma Denise who has provided us with wonderful Bernese Mountain dogs and friendship; Mike Acker, my editor, publisher, and advisor, Sarah Nguyen, for her editing contributions, and Jordann Tomasek, for her assistance with photographs, some of which are semi-ancient. Last, but not least, I thank Blue Pearl Pet Hospital of Tacoma, Washington and Purdy Animal Hospital of Purdy, Washington for the veterinary expertise and compassion they have shown our girls.

All of these generous folks have shared their experiences with our dogs or their expertise with me for this book. Most of all, I thank all the dogs that have enriched my life and the future dogs that will enrich it further. Thank you for giving me the opportunity to share my stories. I hope you enjoy them and come to know and love them like I have.

This book is dedicated to the dogs I have loved, those that have loved me, and, of course, my lovely bride, Sally, call sign "honey badger."

Prologue

THE RAINBOW BRIDGE

A Bernese Mountain dog and a smaller Gordon setter softly pad along a well-worn path through a meadow exploding with colorful flowers. A soft wind rustles their silky black coats. Both dogs wag their tails.

A narrow, white blaze runs down the center of her forehead. Her black, brown, and white coat is sleek and shiny. At first, Peppermander, the Berner, periodically lowers her head and coughs. The black and tan Gordon, Phinneypin, who serves as her guide, stops alongside and gently looks into her eyes, waiting for the coughing to stop. The cough changes to soft pants as the pair nears a bridge crossed by a shimmering rainbow. Pepper's steps become lighter.

They walk with the ease of the gentle breeze, crossing a river on a bridge crossed by a shimmering rainbow. Peppermander looks to her left at Phinneypin. She thanks him for being her guide on her final journey.

As they pass over the river, they see a crowd gathered at the bottom of the bridge. Three smaller female Gordon setters — Abigail, and remarkably named Lori and Lory, stand to the left of the bridge wagging their tails. Samantha, a Giant Schnauzer, stands at the bottom of the bridge next to Tina, a liver and white English setter, and Splash, a rollie polly golden retriever. In the background, a small red dog named Brit jogs back and forth, tail wagging.

All stand ready to meet the one and only Peppermander. The pain of life is now behind her. Pepper has crossed the Rainbow Bridge.

Although the Rainbow Bridge commonly refers to a mythical bridge where grieving pet owners reunite with their fur children, the concept predates modern times. *The Rainbow Bridge: Rainbows in Art, Myth, and Science*, written by Raymond L. Lee Jr. and Alistair B. Frasers, describes how the Rainbow Bridge concept can be found in Australian Aborigine, Cambodian, Chumash, Greek, Hopi, Japanese, Navajo, and Norse mythology.

The Bridge connects the Living Earth with the Heavens, providing a pathway for the transition of animal souls. The concept is so generally accepted by pet owners that it inspired an annual National Rainbow Bridge Remembrance Day, August 28th. Nineteenth-century author Robert Louis Stevenson wrote, "You think dogs will not be in heaven? I tell you; they will be there long before any of us."

As has been said before, I wish the Rainbow Bridge had visiting hours.

Chapter 2

TOUCHED EARLY BY THEIR PAWS

My sister, Janet, and I didn't have dogs of our own during my childhood. My parents were not "dog people," but dogs were nearly always around. The windows of our 1930's second-story two-bedroom apartment in Bellingham, Washington overlooked a yard shared with apartments down the hill.

Standing on my tiptoes, I'd look down the grassy hill to see if the dogs sharing our yard were outside, a boxer and a dachshund! The boxer was lovely. Dark eyes, a furrowed brow as if perpetually in thought, a narrow white blaze on her forehead, a white muzzle, a white shirt, and a fawn coat. She was beautiful and so gentle.

Boxers are among my favorite dogs. They epitomize an appearance of seriousness, but they are filled with kindness. Dachshunds, in my youth, came in more limited colors than we see today, but in two sizes: full size and mini. Standard colors were red, black, or black and brown. They were not the dappled versions we see today, which I refer to as pintos.

My playmate was red with long hair forming a skirt down her chest and fringe on her forelegs. Her nose was pointy, her ears long, and her dark eyes kind. I can see her face almost seven decades later. She had such deep eyes.

Anytime I saw the two dogs in the backyard, I would run out the back door, down the steps, down the hill, and across the railroad tracks. I would remain outside until either the dogs were taken back inside their respective apartments or my mother, Nonie, all pale-skinned 5'2" of her, dragged me back into the house.

My dog friends and I played for hours, running up and down the hill. The boxer would jump up onto her hind feet, darting sideways. The dachshund would chase us as fast as her little legs could churn. They were always gentle. I don't remember being pushed down or being frightened by either dog. Maybe they recognized that I was a toddler and no more than a puppy?

Our play was cut short when we moved to Morro Bay, California so my father, Eddie (renamed "Bompsie" by my lovely niece Angie), could help construct a power plant at Moss Landing. Bompsie was a pipefitter. He was almost six feet tall and dark-skinned due to his Lebanese ancestry. While he was always employed, finding jobs often required the family to move. I hated leaving those dogs, especially when I learned there were no canine companions living next to us in our duplex in Morro Bay.

My parents didn't always like each other because, well, they were married. That is not an entirely fair assessment of marriage. I deeply love my wife, Sally, more than ever, even after 27 years of married badger-bliss.

My parents' marriage was fraught with tension. I was three when my mother and I took the train south to move in with her parents — Grandma Lucy, a very crotchety, former nurse, and Grandpa Henry, a very kind, former carpenter — in National City, California. As if it wasn't enough of a boy's dream to live in a house with a rope swing hanging from a sturdy elm tree in the backyard, my grandparents had a dog! Happy was a collie-shepherd. He was athletic, continually alert, protective, and my constant companion. Tan in color, he looked like he had a white scarf of hair around his neck, extending in a blaze down his chest. A narrow blaze of white extended from the top of his head to his black nose and both forelegs were covered with white sleeves.

Happy taught me many things. Sometimes, by guiding me and sometimes, by just letting me be. He could have warned me when I used a hammer on the front of Grandma Lucy's aquarium to let the fish out to play. But instead, he stood by and did nothing. This didn't end well for the fish. Maybe Happy wanted to see what would happen. Maybe he wanted to see if I would really do it, making the same mistake many have made when they see me considering a foolish course of action. If I'm good at anything, it's following through!

* * *

Eventually, Bompsie found work in nearby San Diego. He joined us in National City and moved us into a small house next to his parents — Grandpa Oscar, a retired pipefitter, and Grandma Nellie, a rail-thin Midwesterner who had been making a living scrubbing hotel floors when she met Grandpa Oscar.

We left Happy behind, but he was only a few miles away. I could still visit when we drove the five miles between the grandparents' homes. No animals lived with Oscar and Nellie. The siding of the house was white asbestos tile, the floor was linoleum, and the interior walls were covered with tongue and groove cedar.

In less than a year, Grandma Lucy and Grandpa Henry left Happy in a kennel while they traveled. Upon their return, the kennel operator explained that Happy had jumped up, caught his collar on a six-foot-tall fence, and suffocated. This broke my heart. Happy was gone. His end seems as implausible now as it was then, but three-year-olds rarely have the opportunity to investigate the death of a dog.

These three early dogs shaped my attitude toward animals. They all showed me kindness. They all showed me companionship. None of them asked for anything in return. They seldom do.

Grandma Lucy and Grandpa Henry inspired my love of reading and my interest and reverence for the living world. Each night, Grandpa Henry read in a chair by the floor furnace through which I could see the blue and red natural gas flames. Their home included a wide variety of books. I had an innate interest in history and the natural sciences. My favorite history book was a pictorial history of World War II which ended only five years before my birth. My grandparents had *National Geographics* dating back to the early 1940s. I devoured those magazines as I traveled to foreign lands or under the sea. All those places were inhabited by animals and/or people that were different from me.

* * *

My parents purchased a suburban tract house in Chula Vista, California where my mother remained until her death at age 94. When we moved to Chula Vista, it was a mixture of citrus orchards, tomato fields, cattle ranches to the east, and houses. Chula Vista is just south of San Diego, home of the world-famous San Diego Zoo.

Zoorama was a weekly television show produced between 1955 and 1970 featuring Dr. Charles Schroeder. Dr. Schroeder was a veterinarian, a zoo director, and my childhood hero. It is rare to meet a childhood hero, much less work for one, but I was blessed with the opportunity to work for Dr. Schroeder toward the end of his career as Director of the San Diego Zoo. I visited with him intermittently over the next 15 years prior to his death.

Many of us do not have the opportunity to realize our childhood ambitions. However, not only did I get to work for Dr. Schroeder, but I also eventually became a zoo director myself. As a child, I wanted to be Dr. Schroeder. I've learned that I am sometimes regarded as too forthright or cantankerous by associates, just as Dr. Schroeder was regarded. He was goal-oriented, very decisive, demanded accountability, and some might say difficult. I am equally goal-oriented, decisive, demanding of accountability, and, some might say, just as challenging to work with.

A seed of an idea was born during those early years of reading about animals and watching *Zoorama*. I wanted to take care of animals, and I wanted to be a veterinarian. But how to get there? I didn't even have any animals of my own except a few aquariums filled with tropical fish, and they were a sore point in the household over which my father threatened repeatedly to move out. I needed and wanted a dog. Needs and wants are synonymous to me; yes, I have not had sufficient behavioral counseling or maybe I did but it didn't stick.

I did not live with dogs for the next 18 years. I begged my parents for a dog, but Bompsie's answer was always the same, "If I wanted a dog, I would have a dog." He was the original Captain Obvious and in retrospect, I inherited his firm sense of the obvious. My mother's answer was always, "We'll see," which meant "Hell no!" in gentle Nonie talk.

I interacted with dogs whenever possible. My close childhood friend from Texas, Keith King, whose father called him "Keithy Boy," had basset hounds in the household. They were named Ooftie and Charlie. My best friend, David Chabner, had a father-son team of pugs, Pudge and Chipper. They took great pleasure in embarrassing his beautiful older sister, Judy, by taking turns mounting each other when she was visited by boyfriends.

A dog of my own had to wait.

Chapter 3

THE SETTERS OF SAN DIEGO, TRAGEDY, AND THE LITTLE RED DOG

The AKC sporting group contains a wide variety of dogs used to assist hunters in the capture and retrieval of feathered game. Spaniels were bred to point and/or retrieve pheasants, quail, and other ground birds. Retrievers such as the very familiar Golden and Labrador were bred to retrieve game on land and in the water.

Pointers and setters were bred to hunt birds in grasslands and woodlands by scent. They would detect birds scent twenty or more yards away and freeze in place. They were still as statues when close to the bird. The term "setter" dates back to the time when the dogs would "set" the bird in place. During this time, the hunter would collect the bird with a net before the advent of the shotgun. Shotguns shifted the odds in the hunter's favor, although sportsmanlike conduct requires shooting the bird in the air. True sportsmen's conduct would require that the birds be armed in a similar manner.

Gordon setters may date back to as early as the 1600s but have existed in their present form since the 1880s. They are beautiful dogs with shiny black coats and mahogany markings for eyebrows, around the muzzle, lining the ears, along their chest, belly, leg, and tail feathers. They appear to be wearing black and brown pants suits. Gordon setters range from 23 to 27 inches in height at the shoulder and weigh between 45 and 80 pounds. Short-backed, they are more muscular than the English and Irish setters. They are very focused, slow, and careful hunters. Gordon setters are outstanding family dogs. They are gentle, friendly, and loyal. They are wary of intruders, and may occasionally have scuffles with other dogs as a result of guarding their family. They are strong-willed, single-minded, easily distracted by any quick-moving small furry or feathered animal, and have high energy and a greater need for exercise and activity than the other setters. These features help Gordon setters successfully compete against other breeds in agility events, except the super-canine border collies which, in my opinion, should only compete against other border collies. Border collies just aren't fair. Ask any other competing breed.

My first big canine break came when I married my first wife, the athletic, lovely, intelligent, and kind, Sharon Stump, on June 20, 1971. Sharon was a wonderful friend who shared my affection for all things living including dogs. Sharon grew up with a Dalmatian with a spectacular name – Domino.

What an opportunity! We were now the adults in charge and decided we could get a dog! But first, we needed a house to accommodate our furry friend. We moved into a 1950s pink rental with two bedrooms and one bath. The house was in Imperial Beach, California, the back yard surrounded by a concrete masonry unit wall, the front yard enclosed by a three-foot-tall white picket fence. It was located just a little over one and a half miles from the beach.

Imperial Beach was dear to me because as a youngster, my Grandfather Henry, my friend David Chabner, and I spent a summer day or two per week fishing from the Imperial Beach Pier catching queenfish (*Seriphus politus*), barred surf perch (*Amphistichus argenteus*), occasional California barracuda (*Sphyraena argentea*), barred sand bass (*Paralabrax nebulifer*), and California scorpionfish (*Scorpaena guttata*). Word to the wise, beware of the scorpionfish's spines. They are venomous, and you will find yourself in serious pain if poked. Local fishermen know them as "rattlesnakes."

Now that we were settled, the big question was what kind of dog did we want? And how could we afford a dog? We had no money. Having no money as a married couple in the 1970s was different than having no money as a married couple today. We *literally* had no money. We ate a lot of macaroni and cheese and Hamburger Helper to ensure we received enough sodium, and we never turned down a free meal. Of course, hamburger and chicken were $0.25 per pound at Mayfair Market in Chula Vista, so we got by. I know we weren't alone at the start of the 70s. Most young people at that time left home upon graduation from high school (no, we really did) and most young people also went to work. At the time, it was the expected progression to adulthood.

By this point, the Vietnam War was well underway. I was attending Southwestern Community College in Chula Vista, California. The draft was in effect and students would disappear overnight from class. It seemed that the Vietnam War would go on until infinity. Student deferments were available, but I did not accept a deferment. It seemed to me that if I was drafted, I was drafted. I considered joining the Marine Corps to fly helicopters even though the life expectancy for Marine helicopter pilots was around six weeks at that time. Two close friends who had completed yearlong tours in Vietnam convinced me that was a poor idea. They were probably right. I joined the military a bit later, 38 years later to be exact, but that is another story. I never was drafted.

Everything I do is a project. I enjoy the research and planning as much as achieving the end goal. Those of you who remember the Sears and Montgomery Ward Christmas catalogs would understand. As children, we poured over the toys in those Christmas catalogs. Usually, we didn't receive many of the items we dreamed of, but the aspect of the selection process was rewarding in itself.

Selecting a breed and finding a dog was a similar process. I'd read books concerning dog breeds for many years. It is a behavior pattern that was repeated later by our younger son, Maxwell, when he had an opportunity to select a breed of dog for a pet. My favorite canine tome was the highly artistic *Man's Best Friend: National Geographics Book of Dogs*, which I still have.

As soon-to-be dog owners, we wanted to meet the breeds in person and see how their behavior matched their written descriptions.

Sharon and I heard about the American Kennel Club All Breed dog shows. It was staged in San Diego by the Silver Bay Kennel Club either in Balboa Park or at the Del Mar Fairgrounds. The earliest Silver Bay Kennel Club show we could attend occurred on March 14, 1971, at the Del Mar Fairgrounds. Two breeds were high on our list of companions: the Bernese Mountain dog and the Gordon setter (aka God's Own setter). Secondary breeds under consideration were long-coated collies, Golden retrievers, German shepherds, and Weimaraners. The collies and German shepherds crossed themselves off our list instantly. They were so barky! The Weimaraners crossed themselves off at the opposite end of the spectrum. They were so quiet and seemed too perplexed. The golden retrievers, as always, were wonderful and one of the very best all-around family members.

As we walked the show grounds twice, we looked for the final two breeds: the Bernese Mountain dog and the Gordon setter. We looked everywhere, but they were nowhere to be found!

Backing our story up a bit, we had never seen a Bernese Mountain dog in person. Well, there was one in a television commercial for dog food with everyone's favorite serious, always honest, always problem-solving father, *Bonanza*'s Ben Cartwright, aka Lorne Green. That was as close as we had come to seeing a Berner, even at our first dog show at the Del Mar Fairgrounds.

About to give up on both breeds, we exited the back door of the giant hall which served as The Hall of Crap during the annual San Diego County Fair. It wasn't officially called The Hall of Crap, and it also could have been called "The Hall of Random Objects" where you might purchase and experience extreme buyer's remorse when you return home. Halls of Crap were precursors to the QVC Shopping Network.

We were walking along when suddenly, a Gordon setter appeared in front of us, pacing toward us with their handler! Not short on assertiveness, we ambushed the handler and learned they were from Scottsdale, Arizona.

"You should speak to Ray and Kay Ruse. They raise Gordon setters and live in Santee, just a few miles from here," suggested the handler.

We tracked down Ray and Kay Ruse and were not disappointed. They were very special folks. Ray was an aeronautical engineer at Solar Industries in San Diego. They had three children and in their spare time, raised Gordon setters with wonderful personalities. They were showing one of their Gordon setters, Lochibar Lochleven, aka Locky to his friends, on the day of this show. Locky was a sturdy Gordon. He was darker than some in muzzle and feet, but he was so stocky and so strong. He had a wonderful personality. The Ruses invited us out to their home for dinner and to talk about dogs. We had Hamburger Helper and potatoes. Like us, they were also frugal.

We learned from Ray and Kay's example that conscientious dog breeders are committed to their breed and long-term care for their animals. They were not concerned with generating profit. Conscientious breeders need assurance that you are interested in a dog for the dog's sake, understand the breed, and do not believe you might gain some indirect increased status from your dog's performance, the sale of offspring, or the price of a stud fee. Typically, responsible breeders like Ray and Kay will ask if anything changes in your life that requires you to rehome your dog that you contact them first. This has been a consistent finding with the dedicated breeders I have met over the decades.

The Ruse family became our close friends. They freely shared their knowledge and passion for dogs with us. Knowledge and passion are priceless. After sharing many dinners with Ray and Kay, they loaned us our first Gordon setter – Abigail! They shared co-ownership with us, but Abigail lived with us. For a time, they loaned Abigail's best friend, a Gordon setter of the same age, Lory, to us. We now had two six-month-old Gordon setter puppies in our little house, and they had each other.

Different as night and day, Abigail and Lory were inseparable. Abigail was more lightly boned and more sensitive. Lory was very much a clown and heavier-boned. Abigail was wary; Lory loved everyone. Abigail's markings were a deep chestnut and the fringe on her forelegs, hindlegs, and tail was short. Lory's markings were browner, and her coat was long. Lory would eat anything. Abigail didn't care if she ever ate, but would not allow Lory, or any other dog, to touch her food! Abigail leaned over her dish, head low. If another dog violated the invisible force field surrounding her dish, her hackles stood up like a Halloween cat and she'd let out a low growl. She protected the food even if she wasn't going to eat it.

I thought, *I am smarter than her. I can come up with some way to get her to eat.* I mixed gravy in with her kibble. Abigail proceeded to lick all the gravy off the food I offered. I mixed in shredded cheese. You guessed it, she ate the shredded cheese but not the kibble it was mixed into. I tried powdered cheese which is called "sprinkle cheese" in our house. She licked the sprinkled cheese off the top. I was not smarter than Abigail, but then again, she was a girl.

When I wasn't working in the JC Penney's stockroom or attending classes at Southwestern Community College, I picked Abigail and Lory up in the 1962 maroon Volkswagen (VW) bus belonging to my close friend, Moses Gutierrez. Moses was at the University of Hawaii on a football scholarship, and he had loaned me his car. Sliding VW bus doors had not been invented. A two-part, split, swinging door was located only on the passenger side. The bus floor was metal, and the only seats were in the front. The van was perfect for hauling sandy dogs from the beach.

Imperial Beach is at the southwest corner of San Diego Bay. At that time, the beach was underused, especially in the winter. It was frequented by hardy surfers often affected by illness resulting from the Tijuana River. Sewage spills into the Tijuana River Estuary and is carried northbound by current along Imperial Beach. But it would take more than the occasional illness, even more than occasional sharks, to deter surfers from a good, uncrowded beach break.

The ocean was in front of us. The Imperial Beach Pier where David, Grandpa Henry, and I fished was to the north of us, and the Tijuana River estuary was to the south (it would later become a protected reserve as part of Border Field State Park).

Waves broke hard on the beach, but the pups had no interest in the water. Instead, as soon as they were unleashed, the girls raced south down along the beach kicking up clouds of sand. On their best days, they joyously rolled and rolled on a dead gull or seal, covering themselves with stink! Thank goodness the VW could be easily cleaned, easier than their long setter fur that is. On the first two beach trips, they ran and ran until they were half a mile or more away. They ran so hard on the beach that their tongues nearly touched the ground. I called them until I was hoarse, but they seemed to have lost their hearing.

The second time they ran without stopping, I changed my strategy. The beach was empty except for the girls and me. There was ocean on one side and nothing but sand and marsh on the other. They ran. I called. They ran some more. I hid behind a sand dune. Moments later, they were by my side, panting and wagging their tails.

They never continued running when I called after that one time. I like to think they were afraid of losing me. I am not convinced that any lifeforms can have more fun than puppy friends at the beach.

A favorite outing took us to a fenced little league field close to the border of Mexico. Two Irish wolfhounds and an Irish setter, Colin, belonging to friends, often accompanied the girls to the field. They would all run and run. The wolfhounds were not really running, but they appeared to be effortlessly bound in circles around the smaller dogs.

Colin had poor judgment. He was constantly pestering the wolfhounds, nipping at their legs when they tried to run full wolfhound sprints. One day, the wolfhounds reached the limit of their patience. One wolfhound picked Colin up by the back of his neck, raised his head with the dog in his mouth, and just before he shook the Irish setter like a rag doll (as if it was a wolf for which the breed was developed to hunt), his owner shouted, "No!"

Colin lived to irritate another day! He did not learn his lesson.

* * *

Abigail and Lory played constantly. They were "cujoing," as we describe rough puppy play. Puppies are so ferocious! Their heads swing side to side, their mouths are open, and their lips are pulled back to show their teeth. They growl and make such a racket, but they rarely leave a mark.

One day, Sharon stayed home from work ill and was resting on the couch. Abigail and Lory each had a bone. *Chew, chew, chew, crunch, crunch, crunch.* Hours later, Sharon woke up, stood, turned her head, and saw that they had been chewing on the maple arm of a rocking chair. She was less than pleased. Of course, that rocking chair, purchased at the Maple Barn in National City, (how do I remember these things?) cost only $69.00 in 1971, but at the time, I was being paid $1.55 per hour. Nonie loved the pups. She took the chair and ordered a new arm. Grandpa Henry attached the arm, and it sat in her living room for decades. The chair did not go to waste.

Lory returned to the Ruse household and eventually moved into what was to be her forever home. Tragically…. An uncaring neighbor poisoned and killed a very kind dog. I like to think Lori returned to me in a different dog suit.

More about that later…

I wish I could say that Abigail, Sharon, and my very first dog lived a long and happy life. However, it wasn't true.

Some may remember the gasoline and beef shortages that occurred in the early 1970s. Gasoline was, allegedly, in such short supply that it could only be purchased in California according to your vehicle's license plate — odd numbers one day, even numbers the next day. Gas lines were long. Simultaneously, for some unknown reason, beef was in such short supply that beef trucks were hijacked on the way to the market. A dog-showing friend of ours owned a beef-cutting business. More than one of his beef trucks were hijacked in Los Angeles.

A pair of dog shows were scheduled in two of the smaller but lovely California towns south of San Francisco — San Luis Obispo on Saturday and Santa Maria on Sunday. My dear Aunt Ruth and Uncle Oscar lived in Morro Bay along the coast, but they were close to these shows. Sharon and I wanted to drive up a day early, stay with Aunt Ruth and Uncle Oscar, and then attend the dog shows. Uncle Oscar said Abigail could stay in her crate in the garage, but I made a bad decision.

Our friend who owned the beef-cutting business, an outstanding English setter breeder and handler, planned to show two of his dogs in each of the shows. He offered to drive Abigail to the shows in his camper. I thought this was a grand idea. He worked a very long day before starting his drive from Chino to the showgrounds in San Luis Obispo

Sharon and I ate breakfast and drove to the dog show. We were puzzled. Our friend's camper was nowhere to be seen. As we watched the English setter classes and the Gordon setter classes, we didn't see our friend, the English setters he was to show, or Abigail. We asked the other handlers, "Have you seen him?"

No one had.

Anxiously, we started south on old Highway 101. Nearing the south end of San Luis Obispo my peripheral vision saw something black and brown along the edge of the freeway.

"I think I just saw Abigail," I said.

"What?" Sharon asked.

I stopped the car and repeated, "I think Abigail is there by the side of the road."

Filled with dread, I slowly walked north. My stomach was around my knees, and my feet felt like lead.

There was no question. It was Abigail. She was on her side, feet slightly bent, with a very small amount of blood next to her mouth. There was no other mark upon her body. Abigail had been running south along the freeway, headed for her home over 300 miles away. Abigail had been hit once and died instantly. Our little bright star that never cared if she ate was gone. We were inconsolable and broken-hearted. We had no idea how Abigail got there, but we had no doubt it was Abigail, even without looking at her collar.

Sharon and I drove south in a daze. We had no cell phones, so we had no idea where our friend was. We had no idea what had happened. Reaching the Santa Maria Fairgrounds prior to the next show, we called his wife at home from a pay phone. He had been in an accident the night before. He was okay, but she had no other details. She had no idea that Abigail had escaped and been killed.

Looking haggard, our friend arrived at the Fairgrounds mid-morning. He shared what had happened. Leaving home very late, he arrived in San Luis Obispo around two in the morning. Noticing his fuel was low, he left the highway and drove down a residential street in his fatigued state and sideswiped a parked car. Before the age of cell phones, a resident called the police. With sirens blaring and lights flashing, the police arrived on the scene. He asked to secure the dogs in crates. Instead, the police placed him in handcuffs. An animal control officer entered the camper to take the dogs to the pound. Abigail darted past him and was gone. Our friend was unaware Abigail had run off because he was handcuffed in the patrol car. He was unaware that she had been killed on the highway. If we had taken Abigail with us, if Abigail had slept in Uncle Oscar's garage in her crate, she would have been with us for her life. She lived her last moments in fear for which I have never forgiven myself for.

In a state of shock, we drove back to Imperial Beach. A coworker had been after us to let his brother take Abigail's half-brother, Arrow, who was living with us. Arrow was the son of Locky, the Ruse's male Gordon setter we met at our first dog show. His mother was Coleen. She was also Abigail's mother, a Gordon setter direct from Scotland. Coleen was one of my favorites. She was only about forty-five pounds, and she'd curled up in my lap whenever we visited the Ruse household. Coleen and Locky had been in different latched, chain link runs. Coleen came into heat, unlatched her run, ran down to Locky's run, and opened the latch. Thank goodness she picked Locky for a date! It could have been a dachshund! Sixty-some days later, a litter was born which included Arrow.

Arrow was a sweetheart. He was my father's favorite dog, but we were broken-hearted. Like many people who lose a dear pet, especially a dear, first pet, we didn't feel that we could keep Arrow when someone else wanted him so much. In our desperate, crushed state of mind, we let Arrow, Abigail's half-brother, go to a wonderful home where he lived the rest of his life with a male Irish setter of the same age.

Like Abigail and Lory, they were inseparable, but in this case, for life. Arrow won, we lost. Desperate decisions made when you are heartbroken, concerning people or any living thing, are seldom the right decision.

It's another regret that I have never let go of.

We were not dogless. The English setter breeders, Lee and Sue Williams, lived in Chino, a dairy and farming community through the mid-70s. We spent many weekends driving to Chino on Saturday mornings. We stayed with the Williams and drove home on Sunday afternoons. Lee and Sue knew dogs. We both learned so much from spending time with them and their dogs.

English setters have been around for over four hundred years, predating the development of firearms. English setters are covered in soft, silky, long hair, and they have faint liver or black spots. Some English setters, called tricolored, have both liver and black spots!

Two strains diverged in the late 1800s: Llewelyn and Lavarack. Laverack English setters are commonly seen in all-breed dog shows. Llewelyn English setters are more commonly seen in the field. They are often shorter but come in the same color varieties as the Lavaracks. English setters are gentle, sensitive dogs, retaining some of the "birdiness" for which they were bred. Like the other setters, the Irish and the Gordon, they are strong-willed, focused, not easily distracted, and more refined. English setters are the most sedate and relaxed of the setters. They are gentle, but they do not want to be left alone. Like all the setters, they are outstanding family dogs. English setters stand twenty-three to twenty-six inches at the shoulder, weighing 45 to 80 pounds.

* * *

Remember, we were poor and were living on macaroni and cheese and Hamburger Helper. However, before Abigail's accident, the Williams loaned us Tina, a female English setter that had previously had a litter. To this day, she is the most graceful life form that I have ever seen. Ballerinas are clumsy compared to Tina. She didn't run, she glided. She was so graceful and so special compared to other English setters that her breeder, Lee Williams, had been offered a blank check for her purchase.

She was also the most sensitive animal I have known; her feelings were easily hurt. I was Tina's person. Upon my return from my construction job in the afternoon, she nearly came out of her skin with joy! Nothing made her happier than curling her 45 pounds in my lap. But it was a challenging time of life for me. I didn't have a clear direction, and I didn't appreciate her devotion.

She was an amazing animal, so the Williams were eager to have Tina finish her AKC championship. Modern anti-flea medication, which interferes with flea metamorphosis from larvae to the blood-sucking adults, but is harmless to dogs, had not been developed. Fleas were a serious challenge in areas without a winter freeze, like Imperial Beach. Dips containing organophosphates or natural pyrethrin required frequent use.

Houses and yards became infested with fleas and required "bombing" with insecticide. Bombing the house was not without risk. The chemicals in the bomb were flammable. Occasionally, houses would explode during bombing when the hapless occupant forgot to turn the pilot light out on their stove or furnace. All this adversely impacted Tina's coat condition, and we did not have the money to support her show career. Lee strongly encouraged us to send her to a family in Golden, Colorado who was committed to showing Tina and had the resources to do so. Reluctantly, living in a state of confusion, we let Tina go to Colorado where she had a wonderful life and show career. I still miss her; it was another poor decision.

Sharon and I remained enchanted with Gordon setters. Champion Macalder Black Watch was a very prominent stud dog in the 1970s. If he showed up at an AKC dog show, the other Gordon setters picked up their leashes, picked up their water dish, and headed to their cars. The Macalder breeders produced fine dogs, and we had brief custody of one of their little females, Wendy, for all too short a time. Upon arrival at the Los Angeles International Airport cargo terminal, which I had driven to many times in the middle of the night to drop off or pick up animals for the San Diego Zoo, we heard frantic barking in a small but gruff puppy voice. It was Wendy. Her crate was carried to the lobby and the cutest little ball of black and brown fur we had ever seen was wagging her tail and scratching at the front of the kennel. She wanted out and she wanted out now!

Wendy was great fun and would have been a wonderful family member. She was fiercely independent. If your tone of voice did not meet with her approval, she'd slowly back up on her short little legs, lower her head, and talk back. It seemed like she was arguing or scolding. Leash training or rather leash resistance began upon her arrival at seven weeks of age. Initial attempts indicated that offers of cookies were not going to gain her cooperation because she had no intention of giving up any of her independence. One day, I watched Wendy through a window. I called her, and it took a few minutes for her to look up. I realized that looking up was not a skill immediately needed by a puppy. Smart as can be, she had no potty accidents in the house. Not one. I miss her as much as if she had lived with us for a decade.

I made another mistake in judgment. Wendy's lower eyelids sagged a bit, exposing the conjunctiva within. I wasn't sure if this was common in the Macalder line because of allergies or if it was due to some other cause. The year was 1973. Telephones had been invented, but the Macalder breeders lived in North Dakota and were rarely available. Answering machines had not yet entered use. We had only recently stopped painting on cave walls. I did what we commonly did in 1973 — I wrote a letter, asking for input.

It was a gentle letter, not threatening, indicating throughout how much we loved little Wendy and how grateful we were to have her in our family. I asked about her conjunctiva. It was met with rage. The breeder took great offense, believed I was criticizing his dogs, and demanded that we ship Wendy back to him immediately. I called and pleaded with him that I met no offense, but he was adamant that she be returned. The dog didn't die, but a part of me died when she left.

* * *

The pain of losing Wendy was profound. It was a busy, disjointed time for both of us. By this point, I was working full-time as a mammal keeper at the San Diego Zoo. I was fulfilling a childhood dream while working toward a degree in zoology at San Diego State University. Sharon worked as a mail carrier but longed to return to school. Her intellect and empathy were not fulfilled as a mail carrier. More importantly, the house was empty without a dog.

There is often a silver lining, or in this case a black and brown lining, with loss. The departure of Wendy sparked a change in my interactions with and perceptions of dogs. Any interest that I might have had in dog shows or dog breeding vanished. I realized much later in life that this metamorphosis in attitudes had, unbeknownst to me, begun with the loss of Abigail, the departure of Arrow, the departure of Tina, and culminated with the departure of Wendy. With this transformation, those dogs helped me find my place in the world at 24 years of age.

Mark Twain once said that the two most important days in your life are the day you are born and the day you find out why you are here. Everyone knows the day they were born or at least the approximate day they were born, but some people never find out why they are here. Sharon and those early dogs helped me learn why I was here. I was here to make the world a better place for animals and people. At 24, I felt the profound pain of losing Wendy and found why I was here. Life has been simple and fulfilling after.

Thank you, Abigail, Lori, Arrow, Tina, Wendy, and Sharon.

Shortly after losing Wendy, another Gordon setter, another Lori, or as I have referred to her, "Saint Lori," came into Sharon and my life.

Why did I call her Saint Lori? Because she never did a single thing wrong other than express wild puppy energy. She never chewed anything up, never had an accident on the floor, and like her Gordon setter successor, Phinney, she asked for little in return. Saint Lori carried me through a divorce from Sharon and was a constant thread throughout most of my marriage to Susie, my second wife. I could count on Lori; we loved each other very much, and many times I looked at Lori and thought I could see the original Lory that lived with us for a few months inside her eyes and dog suit.

Lori originated from Hackensack Gordon Setters, an interesting and admirable kennel in rural New York. Breeds often undergo what I refer to as "drift" from their original type if they have not been used for their intended purpose. For example, the Gordon setter is a hunting dog. However, if being a good hunter does not continue as a breeding selection criterion over many generations, then the hunting drive may diminish or be eliminated. However, individual Gordon setters may retain parts of the original type.

Later, you will read about Annie, the Bernese Mountain dog, who retained the herding drive reflecting her breed's origin. As you will learn, Annie was a natural herder although generations in her line had never even seen a sheep. Her sister Violet was much less a natural herder and her Aunt Padi had zero interest in sheep. Zero.

Hackensack Gordon Setters bred Gordon setters for show and field. Their dogs competed in all breed shows, but they also hunted and had done so for generations. Thus, their dogs stayed true to the original breed vision. Lori demonstrated this later in life. Their puppy-rearing strategy was well thought out and stimulating to the puppies. Puppies are like small children in that the more stimulation they receive while young, the more likely they will develop confidence, flexibility, and problem-solving abilities. The Hackensack Kennel was surrounded by woodland into which the puppies were sent in the morning with an Auntie Gordon setter. The Auntie took them out to explore, hear sounds, smell the wind, chase squirrels, splash in the water, and play in the snow. Afterward, she brought them back to their dam in the afternoon. This amounted to a combination of summer and training camp for the puppies and resulted in fit, flexible, and curious pups.

In anticipation of Lori's arrival, Sharon and I once again drove to Los Angeles International Airport to pick up the puppy in the middle of the night. Unlike Wendy, we could not hear Lori barking in the cargo area. Her kennel was carried to the checkout counter, and she crouched with her nose pressing against the front wire. She was wagging her tail, watching, but not crying or barking.

Lori had the energy of ten puppies! She was a black and tan dervish who raced through the house, grabbing and throwing pillows, chewing everything in her path, and running as if her tail was on fire. 10 or 20 minutes of this chaos was overwhelming!

If let out into the backyard, she continued to race about. She would chase birds, butterflies, and anything that moved while entertaining herself. She was so full of life.

My darling little sister, Janet, lived a mile away with her toddler daughter, Angie, and Angie's father, Jim Harbin. On days Sharon and I both worked, Janet and Angie babysat Lori. Lori gave them no quarter. Perhaps she was inspired by Angie's lesser height. She pursued her relentlessly, pulling on her corduroy pants and causing Angie to shriek with fear. Angie and Janet lived only a block from my parents and sometimes joined us for dinner. Lori met Angie at the door. The tears flowed. The screaming started. Jim snatched Angie up out of harm's way. Jumping up into the air, attempting to reach Angie, Lori always seemed puzzled. Why won't her cousin play?

However, Saint Lori grew out of puppyhood and became a gentle lady dog. I recently asked Angie what she remembers about Lori. She remembers Lori was always gentle and that Lori didn't object if she pulled on her ears a little or if she laid on top of Lori. I don't know anyone today who loves dogs or is kinder to them than Angie. Maybe she learned that from her relationship with Lori? Angie has rescued Staffordshire terriers and currently lives with one of my favorite dogs, Phoebe, an English bull terrier (aka shark on legs).

San Diego has some of the best climates in the world conducive to plants and animals. Our backyard was filled with aviaries containing myriad, brightly colored grass finches from Africa or Australia including African cordon-bleu, Australian diamond sparrows, fire finches, star finches, and strawberry finches. Button quail and diamond doves rounded out the large aviaries.

A pair of black, red, orange, and yellow dusky lories, originating from New Guinea and surrounding islands, occupied a smaller aviary on our covered patio. One of the most beautiful birds in the world, dusky lories are parrots, but not seed-eating parrots. Occupying a specialized niche, lories have brush-like tongues which they use to feed on nectar and pollen. They are probably important pollinators in their natural environment.

The lories did not like Lori, shared name or not. Lories are avian gangsters. They do not like anyone, especially other lories. In mixed species aviaries, dusky lories can often be seen rolling around on the ground, feet entwined with another poor lory whom they are attempting to give a hard bite. Tightly gripping the half-inch by half-inch welded wire caging with their feet and beaks, the lories screamed at Lori, challenging her to come near enough to sustain a good bite. Lori was not impressed. She totally ignored their best efforts at intimidation.

Shortly after Sharon and I parted ways, Lori broke into one of the aviaries in which Sharon placed grain containing warfarin rodenticide. Lori had never bothered the aviaries or the birds, but that time, for some unknown reason, like Snow White and the poisonous apple, Lori ate the poisonous grain.

Warfarin is an anticoagulant and is used on a controlled basis in people to prevent deep vein thrombosis. Warfarin came into use as a rodenticide in the United States in 1948 and was registered for use as a rodenticide in 1952.

Rodents can't vomit. This may sound appealing to those who over-indulge in alcohol and bear the consequences, but the inability to vomit works against rodents ingesting toxic substances. Warfarin disrupts the rodent's blood clotting pathways by blocking an enzyme called vitamin K epoxide reductase that activates vitamin K1. Activated vitamin K1 is necessary for blood clotting. Rodents or humans ingesting toxic quantities of warfarin without therapy, bleed to death internally. According to poison control centers, as many as 10,000 children in the United States each year are treated for the ingestion of rodenticides, chiefly those containing warfarin.

Returning home from work as a hospital keeper at the San Diego Zoo, Sharon found Lori on her side, gray mucus membranes, barely breathing. Sharon rushed Lori to Dr. Szekeres's clinic miles away. Based on the history and clinical findings, Dr. Szekeres concluded Lori was affected by warfarin poisoning. He induced vomiting, confirming it was a warfarin rodenticide by the blue indigestible granules that are placed in rodenticide for identification. He promptly administered the vitamin K, the antidote for warfarin, drained blood from her thorax to help her breathe, administered intravenous fluids overnight, and saved Lori's life. Dr. Szekeres was a wonderful veterinarian. He was Hungarian, with a thick accent, and practical. Upon Dr. Szekeres' retirement, his clinic was purchased by Dr. Brian Golden, a part-time veterinarian at SeaWorld California who later played a different part in Lori's story.

A few weeks later, my mother called me and told me that Sharon had stopped by their house, opened the front door to the house, let Lori in, and walked away without a word. Lori was once again my girl, eventually with a new mom — my second wife, Susie. Lori was joined by Susie's two dogs. Britt, a 29-pound little red dog, and Casey, aka Digger, a female Brittany spaniel who later moved onto a ranch where she could dig to her heart's content.

Lori never really accepted Susie's authority; she seemed to feel that she had seniority and she wished to be called Lori Joseph Joseph since she had to "train" two mothers whose last name was Joseph. This sometimes troubled Susie, but Lori did have seniority.

Gordon setters, and some dogs in general, are, in my experience, aware and astute in their judgment of people or animals they might think pose a risk to their families. Lori readily accepted people, except for all the junior high students who walked by our house each day. Lori recognized junior high students for what they are: dangerous lifeforms, i.e., teen monsters. The other exception that Lori did not accept was the significant other of a young lady who worked with Susie at SeaWorld. Each time the couple visited our house, Lori kept her eye on him, growling occasionally throughout the visit. She did this for no other person. Eventually, the friend and her significant other parted ways. Afterward, it became apparent that he had a substance abuse problem and that he physically abused his girlfriend. Lori knew. We couldn't see the signs, but Lori knew. Was it her keen intuition or something else? I experienced a similar situation with our golden retriever, Splash.

More on that in my next book…

Britt, the little red dog, had a temper and was highly intelligent. I first learned of this while we lived in Lemon Grove, in San Diego's East County. As I returned from work at the San Diego Zoo one afternoon, a neighbor from across the street stopped me.

"Your red dog is in our yard all day chasing our golden retriever!"

"That can't be. He is in our yard every day when I get home," I responded.

Our fence was around four feet tall. Britt was short, but athletic. I walked to the other side of our fence and called, "Britt!" Over the fence he jumped, easily clearing the top wire. I responded by yelling, "Bad dog!" Britt decided this was entrapment and lost his mind. Unable to file a lawsuit, he began furiously growling, jumping up at me, and making attempts to bite me for about 30 long seconds. Fortunately, in my youth, I was not only indestructible but agile. He didn't leave a mark on me. At the end of his anger, he wagged his tail and walked back to the house with me as if nothing had happened. Maybe he thought our coaching session was over. Maybe he thought I had learned my lesson…

* * *

Susie and I left the San Diego Zoo and briefly moved to Durham, North Carolina when I was hired as manager of the Duke University Primate

Research Center. A short time later, we moved back to San Diego and went to work at SeaWorld — Susie in the Animal Behavior Department and me in the Animal Care Department.

Also, that's another story…

Almost three years later, I was accepted into veterinary school at the University of California, Davis. I never really expected to be accepted and was conflicted. I didn't think I was smart enough to go to veterinary school. My full-time position as an animal caretaker at SeaWorld was entirely outdoors where I am most comfortable. Every day, I cared for bottlenose dolphins, harbor seals, California sea lions, Steller sea lions, a leopard seal, sea otters, walruses, and hundreds of stranded marine mammals. Animal care, the ocean, and hard physical work fit me. Days off were spent at San Diego State University working on my master's degree in biology, fishing, or gardening. I was well on my path to continue toward a PhD. and a career in academia.

What to do? Stop my graduate work and go into debt in veterinary school or stay where I was? I needed advice. I approached my graduate advisor, Dr. Neal Krekorian.

"What do I do?" I asked.

"If you stay here, you will finish your master's, go on to complete a PhD., and have a good career in academia. I have no doubt. But every year, you will teach the same courses to students that look younger each year, and will have little time to do your own research," Neal said.

I asked one of my closest friends, Dee Cross, Sea World Animal Care Supervisor (aka Rags because he was a glass half-full person and aka Skeletor because he was improbably thin), "What do I do?"

"You need to look at it this way. If you stay here, you will be promoted, but what will you be doing in four years? The same thing you are doing now. If you go to veterinary school, in four years you will have many more opportunities," Rags said.

I recently reminded Rags of this conversation, telling him, "You were the person whose advice convinced me to go to veterinary school."

"Me?" he asked.

He had no recollection but said he was glad he had given good advice.

Chapter 4

MOVING NORTH TO VETERINARY SCHOOL

Susie, Lori, Brit, and I moved into a duplex in Davis, California, leaving San Diego, the perfect weather, the ocean, and family behind. The other half of the duplex housed five little barky dogs, one of which was a small poodle-like animal named Percy who seemed like the leader of the pack. A motorcycle gang with a fine collie named Maxwell occupied a duplex on the other side. Four dramatic events occurred while we lived in the duplex.

Coming home from a pre-veterinary school embryology class, I walked into the backyard and saw the ground inside the fence covered with oleander leaves and branches, some chewed. Gardeners working for the apartments behind our house had trimmed the oleander and dropped some of the branches and leaves into our yard. Oleanders are drought-tolerant Australian plants that are popular in warmer parts of the United States. The branches, flowers, and leaves contain a cardiac glycoside that causes the heart to race, called tachycardia, cardiac dysrhythmias, vomiting, diarrhea, and sometimes death. Clinical symptoms include dilated pupils and congested mucous membranes.

Growing up in San Diego, Susie and I were aware of this since every child in San Diego is told a story of children toasting marshmallows on oleander branches and dying. Maybe it's true, maybe it isn't, but it's the kind of story that leaves a mark on a kid. Britt's and Lori's hearts were racing! Their pupils were somewhat dilated. We headed to the veterinary school's teaching hospital where they were successfully treated and fully recovered.

The second dramatic event involved Britt and the five little barky dog neighbors. Davis California is warm. We often had our front door open while I worked in the front yard planting sweet peas and zinnias, two of my favorites.

Britt was quietly lying in the front yard when all five of the barky neighbor dogs raced out their front door and attacked him. He was blanketed with little biting dogs. Instantly, his big sister Lori roared out the open front door, grabbed the smaller offenders off her brother, and tossed them aside. After the second attacker had been thrown aside, the rest of the little pack retreated. Britt had been rescued by his big sister.

The third event involved Maxwell the collie. Maxwell often wandered into the duplex to visit with us. He was as fine a collie as you would meet. Susie kept a box of Milk-Bones on top of the refrigerator for Lori. She encouraged both Lori and Maxwell to sit in front of the refrigerator and bark when they wanted a Milk-Bone. Her training was highly successful, (after all, she had been an animal behaviorist at Sea World and was pursuing her PhD. in psychology), but she might agree it was not her finest decision.

Maxwell was a frequent house guest. He would sit in front of the refrigerator, barking until he received a Milk-Bones at which time he returned home. Lori never met a Milk-Bone she didn't like and just sat in front of the refrigerator barking regularly between meals. Britt did not bark at the Milk-Bone God but was pleased to enjoy them at his sister's request. Eventually, the Milk-Bone box was no longer kept on top of the refrigerator. As a side note, our younger son, Maxwell, is named after Maxwell the collie. Maxwell the son knows this.

MOVING NORTH TO VETERINARY SCHOOL | 31

The final dramatic event in Davis involved a slightly different expression of Brit's ethos. Our duplex had two small bedrooms. We slept in one, and I did my best to study in the other. Studying while lying on a bed is seldom a good idea, and it usually ends with the student sound asleep.

Something I did apparently offended Britt. Returning home late from a day at veterinary school, I noticed the quilt on top of the study bed was folded over. This was odd. I unfolded it and found that Britt had pooped on my study site. To this day, I don't know what I did to offend Britt, but I obviously needed to face the consequences.

For our next home Britt, Lori, Susie, and I moved to Woodland and into a trailer on my mentor's farm. Dr. John Anderson was a highly skilled and practical veterinarian at the California Primate Research Center. The trailer was intended to house migrant farmers, and it was located on 40 acres of land between Davis and Winters, California. It was a wonderful, windy, and peaceful place except for the coyotes that came in the evenings to attempt to eat our barn cats.

The cat clowder included Hogan, Rascal, their sister, Shy Cat, and the very short-lived, Fuzzy Underfoot, an orange, unrelated cat who met his demise within days of acquisition on County Road 27. In all our time there, there may have been a dozen cars that drove by on County Road 27 each day. Fuzzy Underfoot managed to find one. Shy Cat followed suit. Go figure.

The coastal hills to our west separated California's warmer Central Valley from the cooler San Francisco Bay coastal cities. Farmland surrounded us. Before today's climate change effects, the area around Davis, Winters, and Woodland, California was frequently affected by very dense fog called Tule Fog. Tule Fog extended from the ground to a height of three to four feet. Nothing was visible within the layer of fog, including the road, but the air above the fog layer was crystal clear. We affixed reflectors at a height of five feet on either side of our driveway. Otherwise, in the dark, we would drive right by our trailer without seeing our turn.

During this time, Susie and I were quite busy (I was working through veterinary school while Susie pursued her PhD. in psychology) so Britt decided there was no reason to remain in our fenced yard. He dug under the fence, creating a large enough hole through which he and Lori escaped. Our closest neighbor was half a mile off. They knew they were our dogs. They knew they were friendly dogs. Did they lure them into the garage, close the door, and call us? No, they called the dog catcher. Apprehended, Brit and Lori ended up in the Yolo County Animal Shelter.

When we were able to pay their bail, they returned home with a kennel cough caused by *Bordetella bronchiseptica*. Kennel cough is a very annoying condition for dogs, characterized by a chronic, dry cough. It is easily prevented today with a readily available nasal vaccine. We had to protect the determined digger, so we tried locking Britt in the trailer during the day. Result: Brit became destructive. Our third attempt at thwarting the escapee was to chain Brit in our barn when we were gone with a chain and not one, but two clips. Why two? He quickly figured out how to undo a single clip!

New Year's Eve, 1982: We drove into Davis to see a movie. Returning from the movies that night through dense Tule fog, we found Britt gone. He had undone both clips. We searched and called the shelter, but no Brit. We never saw him again.

One of two fates was likely his end. We lived in an agricultural area. Sheep lived nearby and sheep owners had a well-deserved dislike of dogs. In my senior year of veterinary school, while on my food animal ambulatory rotation with two of my classmates, the three of us and our supervising Veterinary Resident, Al, rushed to a sheep farm in Winters. Three domestic dogs, all pets, had come onto the ranch. Pack mentality took over and a dozen sheep were killed while another twenty-five were injured. Thus, sheep owners legally shot dogs found wandering on their property. A neighbor may have killed Britt. The other possibility? He may have intersected with the pack of coyotes that regularly came through our farm. I'm still sad about the loss of Britt. He was an interesting little red dog and deserved better.

* * *

As I mentioned before, flea control was challenging in the 1970s and early 80s. The ground did not freeze in San Diego or Davis, giving the fleas year-round activity. Dogs can be so allergic to fleas that a single flea bite causes them to scratch, chew, lose their hair, and be generally miserable. Lori was one of those dogs. Susie took Lori into the Veterinary Medical Teaching Hospital to see Dr. Steven White, the faculty dermatology resident. Dr. White tested Lori by injecting a minute amount of flea saliva antigen intradermally — in other words, between the outer epidermal layer and the inner dermal layer of her skin. Lori's skin immediately erupted with a quarter-sized swelling!

"I have never seen such a strong reaction in any dog," Dr. White said.

Efforts at desensitization to flea antigen failed, but her allergic response was controlled by a daily dose of prednisone which is associated with side effects.

Lori developed some darkly pigmented skin on her belly and plugged follicles where hair should have been. She became somewhat lethargic when she was not defending her little red brother and was gaining weight. Further investigation established she was hypothyroid. Daily oral synthetic thyroid hormone corrected this challenge. Her hair grew back, and her skin returned to normalcy.

* * *

In the early 80s in our veterinary school, dogs were allowed in class. That's not the case anymore. In today's world, if one hundred people think that something like having dogs in class is okay, but one person thinks it is not okay, then dogs can't come to class. At that time, there was less concern about liability; plus, it was a veterinary school, for God's sake! One should expect to see dogs in a veterinary school.

Two blue heelers with separate owners came to class every day when we were not in the clinics. They lay quietly or visited folks in class during lectures. Not only did they not cause any trouble, but they were undoubtedly good for our mental well-being.

Lori didn't come with me to class, mostly because I rode my bike to school. Occasionally, she came along to evening study sessions. One evening, one of my classmates, George Ewing, an incredibly smart student who owned English bull terriers, looked at Lori, looked at me, and said, "It figures."

Lori and I looked at each other.

"I don't know what he meant by that, but I am thinking it was not a compliment," I said.

To this day, I don't know what George meant. If any of you can shed some light on this or, George, if you ever read this, please tell me what you meant. Thank you.

I mentioned that dogs, even if they have not been used for the purpose for which they were bred, may retain some of their breed's behavioral characteristics. Lori was no exception. I don't hunt, but our landlord, Dr. John Anderson, hunted regularly. A pond was located at the back northeastern corner of the 40 acres upon which our trailer sat. Woodland, our trailer's location, is smack dab in the middle of the Pacific Flyway along which ducks migrate from Alaska to California and back again. In the winter, ducks often landed in our little pond to rest during their fall southward migration along the Flyway.

John bred field trial champion Labrador retrievers, the most notable at that time being Tucker. Tucker and John often came to hunt ducks on our little pond or pheasants in our field. Lori accompanied John and the Labradors. Lori pointed pheasants and ducks, retrieving them right alongside Tucker as if she had been trained to do so. She would run so hard and work so hard that she could hardly get up the next morning.

On two occasions, when John was not hunting, Lori ranged into the recently harvested cantaloupe field around our trailer, found a pheasant, pointed it, imperceptibly crept to the pheasant, snatched it in her mouth, and brought it back to me. I dispatched and cooked the pheasants but found them to be less tasty than the chicken from the local grocery store.

* * *

Prior to the birth of our oldest son, Zachary, if I wasn't working at the California Primate Research Center, Susie, Lori, and I would spend most weekends at Frank and Lorraine Sellers' house in the foothills of the Sierra Nevadas, east of Sacramento. Lorraine had been a nurse before attending veterinary school and met Frank while he was undergoing successful treatment for cancer. They developed a wonderful relationship, married, and Lorraine was my "little sister" in veterinary school. What is a veterinary school's "little sister"?

At UC Davis, sophomore veterinary students, i.e., those seasoned veterans who had survived their first year of the veterinary school gauntlet without being institutionalized for life, were appointed as the "big sister" or in my case, "big brother" for an incoming veterinary school freshman. This provides an opportunity for the sophomore student to guide the freshman student through their early days of veterinary school, as there really isn't any other way a person can be prepared. This relationship often continues until the more senior veterinary student graduates and beyond.

Set in a somewhat dry, coniferous forest, the Sellers had a colt mustang that had found its way into their truck's camper on one of their road trips. Having no money, a common theme in my married life, we took advantage of Frank and Lorraine's hospitality, food, and alcohol. Sometimes, Frank and I drove into the forest to cut logs into firewood-sized pieces to split when we returned home. We also planted a wonderful vegetable garden, taking advantage of good soil and lots of sunshine.

Frank and Lorraine left to spend the summer in Australia after Lorraine's sophomore year and asked us to house-sit and take care of the horse. This was a wonderful opportunity to escape the heat of the Valley. My close friend and associate, the dearly departed Dr. Holly Hogan, was accepted into the veterinary class behind Lorraine's and trailer-sat our massive flower and vegetable garden that summer. The only downside was I worked at the California Primate Research Center that summer, which was a 75-minute drive in the morning and a 90-minute or more drive at the end of the day.

Lori gave us a scare while we were in the Grass Valley foothills. Susie, Lori, and I went for a walk in the forest. It was summer and warm, so the rattlesnakes were plentiful. Lori was off-leash because there was no one around. Suddenly, Lori was nowhere in sight! I looked in all directions, calling, "Lori! Lori!" No answer, no return.

Lori had selective hearing. If she was doing something she regarded as important, she seemed deaf. However, if she heard a refrigerator door open or the crinkle of cellophane from the opposite end of the house she appeared as quickly as the Millennial Falcon coming out of hyperspace!

I was panicking! Susie went back to the house in case Lori found her way home. I continued to search the forest and continued to call, "Lori! Lori!" After an hour of calling, there she was with a look on her face that seemed to say, "What?"

I told her that she was the best dog in the whole world, and I was so worried about her. She looked at me with a look that seemed to say, "What are you talking about? I was busy."

LORI JOSEPH JOSEPH, THE MOST PERFECT GORDON SETTER, EVER, IN GRASS VALLEY ON A FOREST HIKE IN THE SUMMER OF 1982.

At the end of my junior year of veterinary school, our oldest son, Zachary, was born. At that time, it was a rarity for graduate students to have a child. In fact, student medical insurance paid for abortions but not childbirth. Zack was around Lori and our barn cats, Hogan and Rascal, from day one. Lori was not truly impressed with Zack. Zack learned to roll before he learned to crawl. He could only roll in a straight line. Zack would roll, stop, look up, and adjust his vector by moving his body. Each time he almost reached Lori, she stood and walked to the other side of the room. She was either being a world-class butthead or just wanted to make sure Zack got his exercise.

Chapter 5

BACK TO GOD'S COUNTRY

Following graduation from veterinary school, I returned to SeaWorld as a staff veterinarian. The lovely Susie also came to SeaWorld where she pursued her graduate research on Adelie penguins (*Pygoscelis adeliae*), and we moved back into Lori's house in Chula Vista near my parents. Lori continued her stellar behavior, never causing any trouble with our boys, Zach and Max, who were just babies.

Lori was the best clean-up dog you could ever meet. Food frequently hit the floor from Zack and Max's highchair trays, but it didn't stay there for long! A vacuum could not have kept the floor cleaner than Lori did. However, she wasn't a counter surfer and didn't eat the boy's food unless they left it unattended on the floor where it was fair game. As I mentioned, she never did anything wrong.

Lori had unlimited trust in me to care for her and keep her safe. I noticed Lori seemed a bit off and seemed to be urinating more frequently. A urine sample was needed for urinalysis. There are three ways of obtaining urine from a dog. The first is to catch the urine in a cup. This method yields some information, but cultured bacteria are questionable as they may have originated in the dog's urethra after the urine has left the bladder. The second is to pass a urinary catheter into the urethra and the bladder. Urinary catheters are commonly placed during surgery or if the bladder has become atonic. This method can push bacteria from the urethra into the bladder, causing cystitis. Using the third method, the dog is rolled onto its back, its belly disinfected midline over the bladder, and a sterile hypodermic needle is inserted through the skin and into the bladder. This allows the aspiration of an aseptically acquired urine sample. This is the superior method because the clinician can be sure that any cultured bacteria came from the urine and not the technique. Today such samples are gathered through the use of ultrasound.

I needed some urine from Lori to take into the laboratory. No one was home. I tend toward the impatient. I picked Lori up, all 60 pounds of her, placed her on the kitchen counter, rolled her onto her back, scrubbed her belly, told her to stay, inserted a 22-gauge needle, and aspirated a urine sample. She didn't move a muscle. Cookies were provided after. More to come on Lori's condition in a minute.

Susie continued working on her thesis research, and I worked 60 to 80 hours per week at SeaWorld. I might have a half-day off every six weeks. Not surprisingly, our marriage blew apart. It was not pretty. There were buckets of tears, angry words, and hurt feelings. I moved into an apartment but could not take Lori with me. I frequently picked the boys and Lori up, visited my parents, and went on excursions.

* * *

Veterinarians can't help but physically examine every animal they encounter, every time they see the animal. I am no exception. I was running my hands down Lori's hind legs when I felt her right knee. It was greatly swollen, twice the size of her left knee, and it felt prickly.

One of the most serious forms of cancer is osteosarcoma, a tumor of the bones. Her significantly enlarged, irregular, bony right knee was suggestive of osteosarcoma. I called Dr. Brian Golden. He was mentioned previously as a part-time veterinarian for SeaWorld, but back then he was also the owner of Dr. Szekeres' practice.

"Brian, can I bring my Gordon setter, Lori, out for a hind leg radiograph? I am very concerned she may have osteosarcoma of her distal right femur."

"Bring her on out!" Dr. Golden said.

Saint Lori required no sedation for radiography. I put on a lead apron and lead-lined gloves. I lifted Lori onto the table and asked her to lie down with her right side down. I gently held her still as Dr. Golden pushed the start button, exposing the radiography film. One of Dr. Golden's veterinary technicians took the plate into the darkroom, turned out the lights, removed the radiography film, and developed it in tanks of chemicals. It was very old school compared to today's digital radiography. Dr. Golden placed the developed film on a vertical radiograph viewer and turned on the light. There, my worst fear was realized, osteosarcoma's typical starburst pattern was easily visible.

In 1987, osteosarcoma carried a grave prognosis in dogs. It still carries a serious prognosis today, but there are more tools and options available. We didn't have the internet, but we had books. I scoured veterinary medical books for information on prognosis. The books confirmed what I already knew: Lori had a poor prognosis. The average survival time for a dog with osteosarcoma at that time was around 45 days.

Why so short? Because at the time of detection, the cancer has generally metastasized, or spread, to other parts of the body such as the lungs and liver. Surgical intervention at the time was amputation of the affected limb, but even amputation and chemotherapy did not significantly increase mean longevity due to undetected metastasis. Lori had mild hip dysplasia so amputating one of her hind limbs would further impact her quality of life.

Lori remained at Susie's house with the little boys and became three-legged lame. After nine months, many times longer than the mean life expectancy for a dog with osteosarcoma, Lori showed the effects of her illness. She was tired. Her appetite decreased. Her general physical condition decreased. Susie and I had a hard conversation. We agreed that it was Lori's time. Not wanting to take Lori into a clinic to release her from the earth, I planned to euthanize her in her backyard.

Taking a friend with me while Susie and the boys were away, I sedated Lori, said goodbye, and gave her humane release. Then I cried and cried and cried. Gently placing Lori's remains in a box, I cut straw flowers to put around her. They were the last strawflowers I grew until this year, 26 years later…

I then drove her to Dr. Golden's office where he agreed to have her remains cremated. It was the Fourth of July 1987. I spent the weekend in my VW campervan in the Anza Borrego Desert. It was the end of Lori's days, but she was not my last Gordon setter.

Chapter 6

ONWARD TO THE MIDWEST

Giant Schnauzers, the largest and most recently developed of the Schnauzers, are one of my favorite breeds. Giant Schnauzers are the bomb! Looking up the meaning of "Schnauzer" will provide a definition such as "a medium or small-sized dog of a German breed with a close wiry coat and heavy whiskers around the muzzle." That is a simple but accurate description. Giant Schnauzers are stocky, square, and muscular dogs ranging from 23 ½ inches to 27 ½ in height. They weigh between 55 and 100 pounds. Samantha was 100 pounds of solid muscle.

Giant Schnauzers were bred by Bavarian cattlemen as large, bold terriers with predictable and serious personalities designed to drive livestock to market and provide protection from predation. They served many early careers including butcher's dog, stockyard helper, and brewery guard, which is probably a very important career in Bavaria. A Bavarian brewery guard is not likely to ever be unemployed.

Around 1900, Giant Schnauzers began careers as police and military dogs, reaching the United States in the 1920s. A Giant Schnauzer's cornerstone is to maintain pack integrity and protect against intruders. However, they are very affectionate with family members, excellent with children, and very trainable. They just need jobs for mental and physical stimulation. They take their responsibilities seriously.

Samantha belonged to Susie, the determined, intelligent, lovely, and provocative mother of my children. Lori, the Gordon setter, had been euthanized due to her terminal cancer, and Susie needed a friend. Samantha was acquired during Susie's and my first separation.

Like all Giant Schnauzers, even as a pup, Samantha was a tank. Our youngest son, Maxwell, was just a baby when we separated. His go-to outfit was Oshkosh B'Gosh corduroy overalls. The straps went over his shoulders and buttoned in front. The inseams even featured snaps to allow easy diaper access. Max wasn't small. When watching a videotape featuring a 29-pound Max at a bit over one year of age, a caretaker can be heard describing him as "gordito." On more than one occasion, Samantha the pup, gripped the front of his overalls, walked backward, and dragged Max across the grass. Max cried. Everyone else laughed.

Samantha moved with our whole family to Chicago when Susie and I reunited. I was hired as an Associate Veterinarian by the Chicago Zoological Society. My lovely wife was hired across town at the Lincoln Park Zoo as Assistant Curator of Birds and Manager of the Children's Zoo.

From San Diego to Chicago is quite a weather change. Our rental house was a two-story carriage house on the north side. A wooden interior stairway led upstairs to the bedrooms.

At 18 months of age, Maxwell was still a bit unsteady on his feet. The tall stairway was challenging, and he often used his hands as well as his feet to climb to the second floor. As I watched him from the bottom of the stairs one afternoon, Samantha sat at the top of the stairs watching his upward progress. Just when he reached the top, Samantha head-butted Maxwell. Down he went about four stairs before he caught himself. No tears flowed. Max was and is more analytical than reactive. Samantha seemed amused and remained at the top of the stairs. She probably could have played bowling the baby all day long. I, however, in a fit of maturity and adulthood, put a stop to this game immediately.

* * *

Samantha and Susie participated in obedience training in Chicago. It was led by one of my friends, Frank Brader, a children's zookeeper at the Brookfield Zoo and the owner of the highest-winning male Rottweiler in the late 1980s. Frank had lost one of his hands as a soldier in Vietnam, but he was an amazing animal handler. He frequently provided physical restraint of a large ungulate while I performed venipuncture, a physical examination, or administered an injection.

Frank also had a wonderful sense of humor. A joke between us that never got old was, "Frank, can you give me a hand with this? Oh, I'm sorry I asked. That was insensitive!"

When Susie first met Frank at obedience class she said to me, "You didn't tell me he only had one hand."

"I didn't think it was important," I answered.

Samantha was highly intelligent and a quick learner. Susie had almost completed her PhD. in psychology, specializing in animal behavior, and had been a marine mammal trainer at SeaWorld. Susie was an outstanding animal behaviorist. That was a winning combination. But there was the bunny test…

The bunny test involved placing all the dogs in the class in a circle where they all sat still. In the center of the circle was, you guessed it, a bunny. It was just sitting there. Samantha quivered; you could imagine that she may have broken into a cold sweat. She may have wanted a cigarette to calm her nerves. She looked around for a shot of whiskey, but she did not break. This was a win for Sam, Susie, and, of course, the bunny.

Chapter 7

MOVING FARTHER NORTH

Chicago was not cold enough for us, so we moved to Minnesota. I was hired as Director of Biological Programs at the Minnesota Zoo. Initially, Susie, now Dr. Susie since following the successful completion of her PhD., worked for me. However, that was intolerable for her as it implied that she might have to comply with something I asked. She quickly transitioned to becoming the senior program officer for the Captive Breeding Specialist Group where she traveled around the globe and led workshops that developed conservation action plans for endangered species and habitats.

Weighing just over one hundred pounds of solid muscle, Samantha guarded her Minnesota home with vengeance. Anyone who knocked on or inserted a key in the front door was greeted with a ferocious display until she recognized who you were. In the winter, with my head covered in a hat, neck covered in a scarf, and wearing a big jacket, I did not open the door until I removed some of the gear and was sure that I was recognizable. A werewolf inside the front door would have protected the house with less enthusiasm. We were safe.

Dr. Annie Seefeldt, a chiropractor who successfully lobbied Minnesota elected officials to change Minnesota state law — such that chiropractors can legally assist animals in conjunction with veterinarians — was, at that time, my Executive Assistant at the Minnesota Zoo and remains one of my closest friends.

Dr. Annie once told me, "Samantha was the first Giant Schnauzer I had known. She was a dear heart, strong and brave. I remember Traci Belting and Diane Fusco referring to Samantha as 'The Schnauz.'"

* * *

Phinneypin was the last Gordon setter in my life so far. It is possible that there might be another female Gordon setter in my future. If so, Maggie will be her name. Did you see how I moved from the "last" Gordon setter to "Maggie" in a few words? Who knows? Count your lucky stars that I am not part of your life.

As you will learn, Phinney's heart was as big as the sky, and that is saying a lot considering all the military working dogs in combat zones, all the law enforcement canine officers, and all the companion animals I have known. No dog that I have known had as much heart as Phinney. No dog that I have known asked for less in return.

Dr. Susie Ellis Joseph, following our first nuclear separation, went through a brief period during which she was fond of me after we moved to Minnesota. Susie knew that I missed our previous Gordon setter, Saint Lori, even though I don't think I whined about it much. Dr. Kathryn Roberts, the Minnesota Zoo Director and one of the most intelligent and talented women I have known, had a little sister named Sarah. Sarah had two male Gordon setters, one of which, MacDuff, was bred in Rochester, Minnesota, the birthplace of the original Mayo Clinic. Susie and I had met Sarah's dogs.

Susie had a brilliant idea. She didn't share it with the boys who would have ratted her out in a second. On Father's Day, Susie, nicknamed Susie Wild Hare in honor of her mother, Granny Wild Hare, informed me we were going on what most people would call a road trip. I referred to it as a Hare Raising Experience because the black and silver Ford Aerostar contained me, Susie Wild Hare, and the two boys. Hare Raising Experiences were usually long drives with vague destinations. Along the way, we might stop at an antique venue. Susie loved the character and craftsmanship of antique furniture. An Experience also included a lunch stop at a roadside diner, few of which continue in existence today.

The stated Father's Day destination was Rochester, Minnesota. We passed through Red Wing, famous for pottery, and, surprisingly, we didn't stop. Nearing Rochester, I heard the challenging command from Susie. "Turn here," followed by, "Turn here."

Why is "turn here" a challenging command? Because it is usually given when the intersection is imminent, or the vehicle is in the intersection. Unbeknownst to me, Susie had tracked down Marie Jackson, the Gordon setter breeder that provided Sarah Roberts with MacDuff, a very tall Gordon setter with a proclivity for eating things that weren't a part of his diet such as nylon stockings and razors.

I didn't know why we were here, but I was used to sketchy or no detail in Hare Raising Experiences. This information was on a need-to-know basis only, and I clearly didn't need to know. The boys had spent the last hour engaged in backseat wrestling and boxing. The destination or length of the journey did not determine if backseat wrestling and boxing were scheduled. If we were in the car, they would occur.

Marie, a fifty-year-old woman, met us at the door and invited us in where we met Phinneypin. Phinney was two years of age and was about seventy pounds with a fine coat, ears that seemed to almost reach the ground, and a wagging tail that wouldn't stop. He was not the largest male Gordon setter I had known. Phinney had been in a previous home which didn't work out. He was Macduff's smaller brother. I vaguely remember that his starter parents may have been divorced. It was not likely Phinney's fault.

Phinney jumped into the van as if he knew it was his ride. He visited with the boys all the way home to meet Samantha. The boys had grown up with Saint Lori, more recently Samantha. They were comfortable with dogs and knew how to play with and love dogs. Dogs were simply and completely members of the family.

"Phinney was the first Gordon setter that I had ever known and was beautiful. I remember that you called him God's Own setter, and I was too embarrassed to ask if that was really what the breed was called," Dr. Annie recalled.

As far as I am concerned, Gordons are God's Own setters.

Phinney ran into the house, met Samantha, and they immediately became great friends! No, they didn't...

The introduction of a new pack member follows an unpredictable path. Introductions can be very simple, just place the dogs together and all is well. Ta-dah! However, they can also be complex, especially with aggressive breeds and dominant dogs. It is often easier to introduce a male to a female or a female to a male rather than to introduce dogs of the same sex because of dogs' attention to social hierarchy.

Phinney was neutered and Sam was spayed. This should be easy, thought the veterinarian, which would be me, and so thought my spouse, a PhD. in psychology who specializes in animal behavior. Furthermore, Samantha got along with all the dogs that she had previously met. Not this time... Sam seemed to know that Phinney was here to stay. She looked back and forth between us, seeming to ask, "Why wasn't I consulted?" Or maybe she echoed the words of Bompsie, "If I wanted a dog, I would have a dog!"

For an entire week, harmless but noisy skirmishes occurred at our home. Phinney might initiate an aggressive chase, complete with barking. Samantha was as likely to do the same, and it was less than playful. Neither would give a quarter. Furniture was upended and children were knocked down.

Well-planned introductory strategies were discussed and implemented. They were placed on leashes. They received rewards only when calm. After a week, it stopped but not likely due to our efforts. They never had another disagreement and became fast friends.

Phinney and Samantha enjoyed their small yard in Minnesota — a green zone of dense woods formed a semicircular barrier at the back of the yard. An invisible fence encircled the entire yard. This allowed the dogs to help in the garage and help with gardening in the front yard without worry of escape. The backyard included oak trees and chipmunks ran between the trees, under the roots, and through hollow logs. The chipmunks were their favorites. Posting at opposite ends of a hollow log or a hole under the roots, they stared at the hole as their muscles quivered with tension. The chipmunk bolted! Off they ran in pursuit. They never caught a chipmunk, never even came close.

Although Phinney was neutered and Samantha was spayed, Phinney thought his big sister was very attractive and that she wanted to be his girlfriend. She didn't since she consistently rejected all his advances. Phinney seemed to have watched the Animal Planet segment in which a male praying mantis or a male black widow spider presents his would-be girlfriend with an offering of a dead insect. We must admit, this is a little gentlemanly. Women must admit that what follows from female praying mantis or black widow spiders after they receive their gift is not very ladylike. For those who do not know, they eat their boyfriends. On the other hand, many human males don't even provide dinner or a movie. Female spiders and women might suggest such human males be devoured.

Phinney didn't offer Samantha an insect, but he offered her what he knew she would find desirable — a tennis ball! Samantha loved to play with tennis balls. During a game of throw-the-tennis-ball, I would throw the ball and Phinney and Samantha would chase it. If Phinney reached the ball first, he would run back toward me with Samantha in pursuit. However, he would stop short of bringing it back.

Instead, he would turn, face Samantha, drop the ball in front of her, and then stand perfectly still. He would face her and wait. What was he waiting for? He was waiting for her to pick up the ball. He would then run behind her and mount her. She didn't want to drop the highly desired ball and couldn't effectively growl and snap with the ball in her mouth. This worked twice. After that though, Samantha was onto Phinney. Thereafter, he dropped the ball in front of her. She leaned forward, the ball inches from her mouth, and stopped. Phinney remained where he was, tail wagging, muscles quivering as if he was pointing a quail. Samantha was a fast learner. She never picked up the ball again. Phinney was a poster child for random reinforcement. He never stopped dropping the ball in front of her nose. Hope springs eternal in males ranging from invertebrates to allegedly evolved humans.

Phinney really didn't believe in the word, "no!" In Phinney's dictionary, "no" meant either "not now" or "not while you are looking." Granny Wild Hare, Susie Wild Hare's lovely, wonderful mother who remained very close to Sally and me long after the demise of Susie and my marriage, came to visit.

Granny was one of the most entertaining, kind people I have known. She liked to cook. Throughout my career of three wives, I have always enjoyed the presence of house guests who liked to cook. Granny liked to cook what was known as "Granny Wild Hare Cookies" which contained oats, chocolate chips, brown sugar, vanilla, flour, and, well, that's all I know. My lovely bride Sally now makes the same cookies from the same recipe, but they are now called "Badger Cookies" in honor of my incumbent, lovely wife.

There is a subtle difference between Granny Wild Hare Cookies and Badger Cookies. Granny Wild Hare was very concerned that the boys did not eat vegetables. The sight of a vegetable on their plate was enough to prompt gagging, if not outright vomiting. Granny was sure that she could improve their diet… by grinding a small piece of zucchini into an enormous batch of cookies. Why did she make an enormous batch? Why does Sally make an enormous batch? Because I can't stop eating them. Don't make them unless you make an enormous batch.

Back to Phinney…

Granny was baking Granny Wild Hare Cookies in our Minnesota kitchen. A window was above the kitchen sink, looking out into the backyard at the bird feeder and the surrounding forest beyond. The boys, as usual, were locked in near-mortal combat in the backyard.

The stove and oven were to the left of the kitchen sink and a counter with overhead cupboards was to the right. Granny removed the cookies from the oven, placed the cookie sheet on top of the stove, scooped up each cookie, rotated 180 degrees to her right, and placed the cookies on brown paper bags located on the kitchen counter.

In olden times, grocery stores provided brown paper bags, not plastic bags. They were extremely useful for cooling cookies. Walking toward the kitchen, I rounded the corner to my left. As fast as Granny placed the cookies on the brown paper, Phinney snatched them off the counter and ate them. He didn't seem to notice or care that they were hot!

"Granny!" I shouted.

She turned and said, "What?"

"Phinney is eating the cookies as fast as you make them!"

Bless her heart, she hadn't noticed.

Phinney loved Granny Wild Hare and her cookies as much as the rest of us. Occasionally, she sent a coffee can filled with Granny Wild Hare Cookies from San Diego. More than once, I left a coffee can of Granny Wild cookies on the kitchen counter, opened the back door, and walked into the yard. Looking back through the glass sliding door, I saw Phinney rolling the coffee can across the kitchen floor with his nose, ears flying behind. He was striking the plastic lid with his forepaws and trying to get at the cookies. He was a clever dog, and very much wanted those cookies! Maybe he thought Granny had sent them for him?

"My earliest memories are of Samantha and Phinney. I have vivid memories of Phinney in the red house, and his capacity to steal food off tables and counters. He was intelligent [and] recognized boundaries. If a boundary was set, he would poke at the boundary to see if it was firm. There was a metal strip, in effect a red line, dividing the carpeted living room from the linoleum in the kitchen. Phinney wasn't allowed in the kitchen during meals or meal preparation. Phinney absolutely knew he wasn't supposed to cross the boundary, but would absolutely cross it one paw at a time, looking up at you like, *what are you going to do?*" Max said.

As Max said, Phinney was a world-class counter and table surfer. His muzzle was just at the right height to subtly snatch food off the table from the unwary. I traveled from Minnesota to Chicago twice per month where I provided veterinary consulting services to the John G. Shedd Aquarium. This necessitated hiring a sitter to watch the boys, along with Phinney, and Samantha. I went through a lot of sitters due to a combination of the boys' nearly continual warfare accompanied by Phinney swiping any food the sitter was attempting to eat while the sitter broke up the current skirmish. Sitters frequently burst out the front door upon hearing my car enter the garage. They would leave a note on the counter describing the boys' shortcomings and my shortcomings as a parent.

The poor sitters had eaten nothing in two days due to Phinney's surfing ability, and they were never coming back.

"Phinney was a ridiculous dog, always stealing food off the table. I recall you told us that Phinney had a side job as a rocket scientist and left the house during the day to work at NASA. I believed it," Dr. Zack said.

With time, Dr. Zack learned that parents lie. Now a parent of a toddler, Dr. Zack has likely started lying to his son, Ethan. It is the way.

* * *

Our Minnesota house butted against a green belt filled with trees and brush. I was in a constant battle on behalf of my perennials. The forest provided Samantha and her Gordon setter brother Phinney endless entertainment in the form of deer that would stand just out of reach on the other side of the Invisible Fence, making deer faces. Plus, there were also squirrels and chipmunks.

Phinney checked the Invisible Fence daily to make sure it worked. Samantha respected the fence except when there was snow on the ground. Since we were in Minnesota, snow is frequently on the ground in Minnesota, and a lot of it. The snow attenuated but did not completely mitigate the signal to Samantha's collar. It was just enough that if I weren't watching her, she would walk over the buried wire and trigger an electrical shock. Samantha was tough!

She would shake her head from side to side as her collar delivered slight shocks, but she kept going. This required me to put on my down coat, gloves, boots, and a knit hat before grabbing her leash and walking into the surrounding neighborhood to find her.

"Watching Samantha walk through the invisible fence, she barely shook her head with each shock. I imagined that she just decided that is what she would do and cursed back at each shock!" Dr. Annie said.

She never went far though. She just wanted to explore.

A favorite behavior Samantha began as a pup and continued until our last goodbye was laying on my chest, nose to nose, as I laid on my back on the ground. This was not a challenge when she was a twelve-pound pup, but when she was a one-hundred-pound adult, my breathing was a lot more challenging. I loved every minute with Samantha. There is no price tag for that kind of love.

Chapter 8

PHINNEY LOSES A SISTER, BUT GETS TWO BROTHERS

People frequently ask me, "What is the best family dog?"

I always reply, "Tell me about your family. What do you expect from your dog? Have you ever had a dog before?"

Often, this is their first dog. After listening, if they are an active family with children and a yard, I suggest a golden retriever or a Labrador retriever. Why? Because both breeds are patient, forgiving, intelligent, and will be whatever the family needs. They can be couch potatoes or hikers. They can sleep on the bed or sleep on the floor. They are athletic and strong, but not driven like a Belgian Malinois or a border collie. These characteristics have made them a common choice as service dogs for organizations such as Guide Dogs for the Blind.

Golden retrievers are especially affectionate with family members, get along with other dogs, are accepting of other people, and strive to fit in. Golden retrievers originated in England in the 1860s. They are derived from an intelligent and independent breed that had tended sheep in the Caucasus, a mountain range at the intersection of Europe and Asia.

Golden retrievers have frequently been used as hunting dogs on land and in the water where they are kept warm with their water-resistant coats. They are, from my perspective, a medium-sized dog. They range from twenty-one and a half inches tall and weigh between fifty-five to seventy-five pounds, unless, of course, they have been inactive and allowed to become a fat orange carpet.

After Susie moved into a separate house at the termination of our marriage, which made the Death Star's destruction of Algernon look like an episode of a typical home improvement show, she took Samantha along. Phinney, the boys, and I lived together. Samantha wasn't consulted and did not support this decision.

"Samantha hid in the closet at my mom's house when I played the saxophone in middle school. I didn't blame her," Dr. Zack said.

However, Susie traveled half the time to faraway places conducting her conservation workshops. During her absences, Samantha stayed with Phinney, the boys, and me.

My nearly lifelong friend, Traci Belting, remembers, "When my son, Kevin, was a toddler he was the same height as Samantha and Phinney. When we came to visit, Kevin got stiff as a board and scrunched up his nose and eyes as the dogs pushed into him and licked his face. When the dogs lost interest, Kevin went on his way without a word."

Kevin is now grown and has a nice, large dog named Scooby. Apparently, he wasn't permanently scarred by the experience.

* * *

Zack and Max each wanted a dog of their own. Zack wanted a golden retriever. Max wanted a rescue greyhound. I mentioned Zack wanted a golden retriever to my good friend, Pam Herman, the first marine mammal trainer hired by the Shedd Aquarium. She had known the boys from when we lived in Chicago, and I was a veterinarian for the Chicago Zoological Society.

Pam left the Shedd Aquarium and worked part-time for a small animal veterinarian somewhere in Wisconsin, close to Chicago.

Pam called me on a Friday evening and said, "Hey, I think we have a golden retriever puppy for Zack."

"Tell me about it. Pam," I answered.

"He is a seven-week-old farm puppy from Wisconsin. His owner brought him in for his immunizations. He had roundworms and a heart murmur. They took him home and brought him back two hours later. They said he was too much trouble and they wanted us to put him to sleep. My boss said he wouldn't do that, but he would take him and find a home for him."

"Okay, we will drive down in the morning and pick him up at your house in Brookfield."

Zero dark thirty came. Zack and Max loaded up in our blue Ford Probe, and we headed southeast for a five-hour drive to Chicago. Arriving in Brookfield, we met the troublesome golden retriever at Pam and her husband, Mark Ryan's, home. He was a gorgeous bundle of love, and he was the quietest seven-week-old puppy I had ever met, all tail and tongue wagging.

"We stayed overnight with Pam and Mark Ryan and watched *Aliens* on laser disc which represented the highest technology of the day," Max said.

We thanked Pam and Mark then headed back home for another five-hour drive.

Phinney met us at the front door. *What is that behind you?* he seemed to ask. Poking it with his nose, sniffing carefully, he thought, *Oh, it's a puppy!* Phinney was smitten with his new little brother.

It was bath time for the boys when we arrived home. Zack was first. No, it wasn't Zack first. It was the puppy and then Zack. The puppy jumped into the bathtub. Zack and Max laughed. The puppy laughed. Water was on the bathroom floor, the bathroom walls, everywhere.

Phinney came to the door and looked in with his tail wagging. Even Phinney laughed.

"His name is Splash!" Zack shouted. There was water everywhere.

"When Splash entered the household, we stepped up from two to three dogs when Samantha was over, which was half the time. It seemed like a lot of dogs, but I liked it. Splash was clearly bonded to Zack, and Zack frequently dressed Splash up in sports memorabilia. They wore the same size," Max said.

Splash was an unusual puppy. He was continuously calm. His heart murmur mysteriously disappeared. He was very easy to housebreak. He liked to read, and he liked indoor gardening. If I couldn't see him upstairs where our bedrooms were located, I would head downstairs to look for him. I might find several books off the shelf with torn pages. I might find uprooted houseplants and dirt spread across the rug. It was impossible to get angry with him. He was just too cute. We all loved him, including Phinney.

Alas, he was banished from Susie's house for piddling on a pillow or the floor once when I was out of town. I am pretty sure Splash might have uttered the term "broom rider" when he received this information. From that day forward, Samantha stayed with us when I traveled, but Phinney and Splash remained at home with the wonderful dog sitter, Jenny Beem, who continues to raise therapy dogs in Minnesota, or Amy Kizer who has been Dr. Amy Kizer for many years. Jenny and Amy loved Phinney and Splash, and they loved them. Jenny frequently took them to outdoor restaurants by lakes when she was dog-sitting the fur children.

Winter came. Splash didn't like winter in Minnesota. I didn't like winter in Minnesota. It snows in Minnesota, a lot. Sometimes, it would start around Halloween, but it always does by Thanksgiving. It keeps snowing, usually through March Madness, but sometimes until May. Each morning, Phinney and Splash were led downstairs and let outside to go to the bathroom. Falling snow? Phinney headed out and did his business. Splash stood in the doorway. He just stood there staring at the snow. He seemed to say, *that's ok. I will just hold it.* Sometimes, he would hold it for twelve hours or more, which was very strange for a puppy.

Greyhounds are an ancient breed. They were kept by Pharaohs. There's a five-thousand-year-old tomb painting that features a greyhound-type dog chasing an antelope. Greyhounds are a coursing breed that runs down prey using speed and physical endurance. They are slender running machines that come in almost any coat color with delicate ears, an arched neck, and a pointed muzzle. Similar dogs were used for hunting by nobles in Greece, northern Europe, Persia, and Rome.

Standing twenty-seven to thirty inches tall at the shoulders and weighing between sixty and seventy pounds, greyhounds are good-natured but sensitive. They are affectionate with family, good with children, and interact well with other dogs. When their eyes fix on perceived prey, even if it is across busy streets, their focus is locked. They seem to lose their hearing along with their other senses, even defying an Invisible Fence as they pursue their perceived prey. Owners must be constantly watchful.

"When you said I could have my own dog, I read every dog book that I could find and decided that I wanted a greyhound," Max recalled.

Maxwell Benjibuns, six or seven years of age at the time, wanted a rescue greyhound. I sympathized with Max. His mom was gone. She was not very far, just two miles, but she was still gone. A dog of his own seemed like something that might be helpful to a child who seemed a little, well, lost.

Greyhounds are interesting animals. My first experience with greyhounds was at the Caliente Racetrack in Tijuana, Baja California. My paternal grandfather, Grandpa Oscar, was formerly one of Pancho Villa's banditos. He loved betting on dog and horse racing. I am not making the bandito part up either. I am certain they kicked him out of the band for displaying unethical behavior and being too violent...

During the horse racing season, he drove daily from National City to the Caliente track. At the conclusion of the horse racing season, Grandpa Oscar continued daily to the greyhound races. When I was eight years old, Grandpa Oscar picked me up and off we went to the greyhound races in Caliente. I had no idea what to expect, but I thought *this would be fun.*

The greyhounds, wearing colored numbered jerseys, lined up horizontally in individual chutes across the track. At the sound of the buzzer, the greyhounds were released, racing around the track in pursuit of a mechanical rabbit. No dog can run as fast as a greyhound. They run like mindless missiles on radar lock. They see nothing else as their vision locks on their prey. Unfortunately, it was the last time my dear mother allowed Grandpa Oscar to take me to Caliente. I think she feared I would become a desperado.

Greyhound racing began in Wisconsin in 1990 and continued through 2009. At one time, there were as many as five tracks in Wisconsin, one of which was the Wisconsin Dells Greyhound Park located in Lake Delton, Wisconsin. Today, dog racing is illegal in 42 states. They only remain legal in Wisconsin, Iowa, Texas, Alabama, Arkansas, Connecticut, and Kansas; however, the two remaining active tracks are in West Virginia. Over time, greyhound racing has decreased globally. Racing greyhounds largely live lives of confinement and injuries are common. Very few racing greyhounds retire at the end of their racing career.

Loading the boys into our navy blue Ford Probe, we headed to the closest greyhound racing track hosting an adoption program. The track featured an adoption room with a plate glass window facing the track.

"I clearly remember the short, gray carpet in the adoption center located at the Wisconsin Dells Greyhound Park," Max said.

"I remember Rumor drinking a can of Sprite!" Zach exclaimed.

We saw greyhounds on leashes being led to their racing chutes. Would-be adopters milled around in the adoption room as half a dozen greyhounds entered the room.

The greyhounds did not act like the dogs that I had known. They ignored each other. They didn't sniff each other. I thought, *huh*! I then realized the social drive, the pack drive, and part of the basic canine behavioral blueprint was bred out of the greyhound by necessity. If typical dogs raced against one another, they might chase each other, stop, sniff each other, bark at each other, or any or all combinations of these behaviors might happen when they were released from their chutes. The result? Race over!

The greyhounds also ignored the visitors. Greyhounds have been bred for one purpose: to hunt by sight. They were not bred to herd the flock, protect the flock or the owner, enter the burrows of rodents or badgers, or lie quietly at the feet of the owner. They were bred to run and hunt by sight.

Back in the adoption room, I noticed handlers leading other greyhounds to their chutes for a practice race. This was not surprising since we were at a greyhound track. What was surprising was the greyhounds in the adoption room all walked to the window, stood side-by-side, and watched the greyhounds race down the track! Who would have guessed that they were not only participants but also spectators?

Max picked his hound. It was a black greyhound, nearly as tall as Max's six-year-old shoulders, and had pattern baldness across his back that occurs in greyhounds. He was named Rumor, and he was long, lean, and rangy with a typical pointed snout.

Reading Rumor's history, he was available for adoption because he was "too slow." All the greyhounds that were up for adoption were "too slow." Rumor had one more black mark on his record.

He was first adopted by a family that ran a house ape zoo, I mean, a daycare center. Rumor had nipped a child. No information was available concerning what provoked the bite, but Rumor was returned to the track. Max and Zack had lived with dogs since the days they were whelped, I mean, born. It seemed that if Rumor might fit into any household, it was ours, and Max was in love with Rumor. Rumor came home with us, opening the door for one of my most significant failings as a dog owner and parent.

Phinney met Rumor at the door when we came home. He was not impressed and walked away. Splash, still a pup, walked up to Rumor, wagged his tail, and Rumor bent down and licked Splash. Splash had a new friend.

Things went well for the first few weeks. The dogs all got along well until the infamous popcorn incident. The boys were at their mother's, and I was home with Phinney, Rumor, and Splash. On my nightstand sat a large bowl of popcorn. I left the room for some reason and returned to find Phinney buried face-first in the popcorn. I pulled him away from the popcorn and told him he was the worst dog in the world.

Phinney responded by redirecting his frustration in Rumor's direction and the fight was on. Phinney was fearless until the day he died. He never recognized that he really wasn't a warrior. He fell victim to the classic untruth first inspired by Mark Twain: "It's not the size of the dog in the fight, it's the size of the fight in the dog." This could be true sometimes, but the size of the dog in the fight usually matters. It was a mismatch. Phinney was humbled, the fight was brief, but there was a lasting effect. Thereafter, Rumor watched Phinney like a raptor, especially if Phinney approached Splash. Immediately stepping up, lowering his head, Rumor let out a low growl of warning to Phinney who appeared to mean no harm.

Although this skirmish was not a deal breaker, it resulted in a management challenge. I was afraid to leave Phinney and Rumor together in the house while I was at work. I first locked Rumor in Max's room where he slept. I returned four hours later to make sure everything was all right, and I found the inside of Max's bedroom door deeply scratched. There were hundreds of scratches that I would have attributed to a werewolf if I didn't know Rumor was in the room. I hired one of our Zoo carpenters, Carol, to come and repair the door.

Step two was to confine Rumor to the laundry room. How much damage could he possibly do to the laundry room? Walking down the steps to the basement, I turned left and saw Rumor's head and neck extending through a ten-inch diameter hole in the wall. He had managed to work his way through two layers of sheetrock. A total failure on my part. I needed Carol the carpenter on speed dial and could barely pay my bills without correcting damage by Rumor.

Step three was to confine Rumor to a very large VariKennel. I returned home at noon to take him for a walk then returned him to the VariKennel. Rumor became a self-mutilator. I was not giving Rumor what he needed. I was failing and stretched very tight caring for two little boys and working two jobs. I was at my wits' end and not thinking clearly.

I explained to the boys that we could not make Rumor happy, and he was to return to the track. Max was in tears. Rumor was the only thing that he could call his own. Rumor slept with him every night.

Perceptive for a five-year-old, Max said, "They will put him to sleep if he goes back to the track. He has already failed in one household."

Knowing he was correct, Max quietly walked Rumor to the car.

"The short time Rumor lived with us and had to leave was a very pivotal time for me. I read books to him from the library as he lay on my bed with me. It was very hard on me when Rumor went back to the track," Max recalled.

"Rumor had severe separation anxiety. Drugs that are available for companion animals today might have helped him," Dr. Zach said.

"I remember how sad you were [and] how hard it was for your heart when you knew the situation wasn't going to end the way anyone would want it to end. It was a difficult lesson. You can't give everything over to the situation if an animal is in danger of injuring themselves and destroying your dwelling," Dr. Annie stated.

Thank you, Dr. Annie. To this day, this remains one of the largest, saddest failures in my life. I let Max and Rumor down.

Chapter 9

MOVING TO THE PACIFIC NORTHWEST

Susie and Samantha moved to Strasburg, Virginia with Susie's final husband (maybe?). He was my good friend Dr. David Wildt, whom I had known and worked with years before at the National Zoo in Washington, D.C.

Dr. Dave was one of the world's foremost non-domestic animal reproductive specialists. He participated in the development of embryo transfer technology to save endangered species such as cheetahs, pandas, and tigers. I assisted Dr. Dave in some of his projects while serving in a veterinary preceptorship at the National Zoo in Washington, D.C. during my senior year of veterinary school.

During the time of my preceptorship, the lovely not-quite Dr. Susie remained in Woodland with baby not-even-close-to-being-Dr. Zack, although he had been to the veterinary school. Several years later, when our veterinary assets at the Minnesota Zoo were slim, I anesthetized Siberian tigers, enabling Dr. Dave to transfer embryos as part of the Siberian Tiger Species Survival Plan.

Later, I organized a conservation action meeting to save the Chinese river dolphin and invited my lovely soon-to-be-divorced wife Susie because of her ability to manage subject matter experts and cooperatively develop action plans for endangered species. I invited Dr. Dave because of his expertise in endangered species reproductive physiology. It was a gift when Susie married one of my friends and associates to be my boys' stepfather. That doesn't happen often.

Susie and Dr. Dave lived in a two-story gray colonial-style home in a lovely forested area with large grassy areas and perennial flower beds. They were within walking distance of the Strasburg River, and there were plenty of bears and deer for Samantha to keep from the yard. The boys lived with Susie in the summer and with me in Minnesota during the school year. Summers were lonely for me.

I unexpectedly accepted a position as Chief Veterinarian/General Curator at the Point Defiance Zoo and Aquarium in Tacoma, Washington. I planned a move from Minnesota to Gig Harbor. Moving is challenging for anyone, but I had to tell Susie I was moving. I am not afraid of being in the water with killer whales or sharks or immobilizing full-grown polar bears, but Susie was a different story! She can be harsh! She is a badass, but in a good way mostly.

This meant the boys would fly farther to see their mom, which meant they would have more time to fight on the airplane. The boys were very upset. They had lived in Minnesota for six years. Zack completed first through sixth grade, and Max completed third grade. Susie was less than pleased, but Dave was the voice of reason. Susie was often less than pleased with my decisions, but then, we were married at one time. However, one person in the household was glad to see me. Samantha was ecstatic, wagging her stubby little tail and smiling. Each night during the visit, she slept next to me in the downstairs guest room. We had some wonderful, shared memories from our years in Chicago and Minnesota. If I lay on the floor to watch television, she laid upon my chest and panted in my face, just like she had always done.

My visit corresponded with Susie jetting off somewhere in the world to do something important on behalf of animals, leaving Dave, Max, Zack, Samantha, and me to hang out for a few days. In the morning, we went to a local diner. Local folks did not seem to be aware the Civil War ended since Confederate flag decals and flags were everywhere. Diners in restaurants wore Confederate uniforms. I came to understand that Civil War enactments were popular in the area. In the afternoon, the boys and I toured the Strasburg Civil War battlefield. Although this was prior to my military service, it was one of the most sobering experiences of my life to walk where young men on both sides bled, been maimed, and died. I could feel their ghosts. War is so wasteful of the young and the innocent.

* * *

No medication is without side effects. Two years after my visit, Samantha was treated with antibiotics for a urinary tract infection for a prolonged period and developed an associated autoimmune-mediated illness. Her body's cellular defenses were confused; they were attacking her tissues. Susie called me since I was a veterinarian and Samantha's first dad.

"Susie, this is an emergency. It is outside the skill set of your local veterinarian," I said.

Susie agreed and Samantha was transferred, barely alive, to a specialty clinic closer to Washington, D.C. where they could provide round-the-clock care. She could not eat and lost weight, but she was alive and was sent home after a week of hospitalization.

Our shared joy in her recovery was short-lived. As she transitioned to feeding again, she developed a gastric torsion. Gastric torsions are a canine emergency. Occurring more frequently in deep-chested breeds, the stomach twists on its axis, preventing the stomach's contents from moving into the duodenum. This also prevents eructation, which is a fancy veterinary term for burping. The gastric lining continues to secrete fluid. Digestion and bacterial digestion produce gas and the stomach swells like a taught balloon. The balloon-like stomach puts pressure on the vena cava which decreases the return of blood to the heart. The stomach puts pressure on the lungs, thus making it difficult for the animal to ventilate. Acid-base disturbances occur. The gastric lining becomes devitalized from lack of blood supply and stretching. The dog goes into shock, which is a life-threatening emergency.

Sam was rushed to the emergency room in critical condition. The veterinary practitioner felt that she did not have the reserve to recover from the necessary corrective abdominal surgery. She was weak. She was anemic from her illness. Susie called me and asked me to discuss the case with the emergency veterinarian. I concurred since he knew his stuff. Samantha was unlikely to survive the surgery and recover after her serious illness that ended just days before. I broke the news to Susie that it wasn't fair to put Samantha through another surgery from which she was not likely to survive.

It wasn't the first time I made Susie cry, but I think it was the last time. I cried too. We loved that dog.

* * *

At forty-two years of age and twice divorced, I was over relationships, at least with women. I was crispy. For a visual, imagine Anakin Skywalker when he drags himself out of the Lava River. What happened to Anakin was just a scratch. A band-aid and ibuprofen and he would have been just fine.

My hands were full with two jobs, the fewest jobs I had in the previous eight years, and two boys. The lovely and intelligent mistress of black and white, Sally LaTorres, an elephant keeper at the Point Defiance Zoo and Aquarium, made the mistake of coming to a party at our rental house and never going home. It could have been more than one rum and Dr. Pepper or she could have thought that because I was a veterinarian, I had money. Or maybe she was in it for Phinney and Splash. We'll never know. We had known each other and worked together for two months. I thought she was quite a darling. She still is quite the darling, the best wife I have ever had. No, that is an understatement. The best wife anyone has ever had.

Coworkers tried to drag her out the front door at the party's end. They thought this would end poorly, and they would be left with a mess to clean up, something in the order of the Boston molasses flood of 1919. It's always fun until the running, screaming, and crying starts!

She wouldn't leave. You can't make a honey badger do anything they don't want to do. A week after she stayed for the party, I left her with the little angels while I worked in India for two weeks. So, there she was, staying with two very poorly behaved boys, aged nine and twelve. They were poorly behaved because they lived with a single parent who worked multiple jobs, a Gordon setter, and a golden retriever. Even after enduring their madness, she stayed. Let's look at Hercules' twelfth labors for comparison:

Slay the Nemean lion – he whacked it on the head and strangled it; this was nothing compared to getting the boys ready for school.

Slay the nine-headed Lernaean Hydra – Hercules got his nephew, Iolaus (literal translation Bob), who barbequed each stump after Hercules cut off the head; this was way easier than having the boys eat their breakfast without one of them cracking the other over the head with the phone. Note: This really happened while I was gone.

Capture the Ceryneian Hind — He caught a deer, big deal.

Capture the Erymanthian Boar — He caught a pig; it was probably a guinea pig, at worst a Vietnamese pot-bellied pig.

Clean the Augean stables in a single day — Big deal that he cleaned up after horses. Have you ever cleaned up after nine and twelve-year-old boys? Plus, Sally cleaned up after the elephants. No contest.

Slay the Stymphalian bird — This is so made up. Man-eating birds? They were probably just big parakeets, but have you ever been bitten on the cuticle by a parakeet?

Capture the Cretan Bull — He caught a boy cow. Big deal. He probably just had it follow a bucket of grain. Have you ever tried to get two little boys to go to bed?

Steal the Mares of Diomedes — Here Hercules goes with his grain bucket again… Try to get a nine and twelve-year-old boy to clean their room.

Open the girdle of Hippolyta, queen of the Amazon — Did you see the movie *Wonder Woman*? No way Hercules or anyone else messed with her girdle. Try finding out when kids' school projects are due other than at eight in the evening on Sunday night. That's a task!

Obtain the cattle of the three-bodied giant Geryon — Three bodies tripping over themselves.

Steal three of the golden apples of the Hesperides — He picked some apples. Big deal, they fall off trees.

Capture and bring back Cerbus — This is exaggerated. Cerbus was in reality a mini-dachshund. Sally had to take care of Phinney and Splash.

Sally's tasks were much harder than Hercules'. We won the lottery.

The same night that Sally came over (and never went home), Phinney made the evening memorable. This story illustrates the mindset typical of folks with careers in animal care. The animal keepers, the Zoo Director, the Zoo Deputy Director, and the Director of Development were all at the house. It was a potluck. The kitchen counter was covered with various food items that folks had brought along.

Our good friend, Rhonda Wilcox, had brought an apple pie — the kind with the cross-hatching crust on top. I looked over and saw that Phinney had his front paws on the kitchen counter and was munching away at Rhonda's apple pie. It seemed as if there were no Granny Wild Hare Cookies around, so he settled for Rhonda's apple pie. I would take this as a compliment, Rhonda.

"Phinney!" I yelled in the very same way I had yelled when Phinney had his head in my popcorn dish in Minnesota.

Everyone turned to look! With his paws still on the counter, Phinney turned and asked, "What? Can't you see I am busy?"

"Get down!"

Phinney dropped to the ground, but he had his share of the pie. People in many vocations would have discarded Rhonda's pie or cut away the part that he may have slobbered on, but the Zoo folks ate the pie. It was very good.

Thank you, Rhonda, for making the pie, and thank you, Phinney, for leaving us a little.

Phinney fulfilled an important role in my life and played it well. Phinney guided me through this transition. He lived with me during the end of and after my marriage to my lovely former wife, Susie, and guided me through that difficult time. He never slept on the bed, he slept on the floor immediately by the bed, facing the door. He transitioned me, the boys, and Sally to the formation of our newly formed family unit.

During the few months that Sally, the boys, Phinney, and Splash lived in a rental house in Gig Harbor, Splash decided he needed to investigate something under the back deck. He crawled several feet under the deck but was perplexed about how to get out from under the deck.

"Phinney came into the kitchen, whined, went to the door, came back, and whined until I followed him outside to help," Sally said.

Sally went out into the backyard.

Phinney was crouched, looking under the deck shouting, "Splash is stuck under the deck! Splash is stuck under the deck! We must help him, or the spiders will eat him!"

Phinney may have said all of that, but all Sally understood was that Phinney was agitated and, indeed, Splash was stuck under the deck. No amount of pleading could inspire Splash to turn around or back out the way he went in. He had accepted his fate. He would die under the deck and be eaten by spiders. With one exception, Splash was a fatalist throughout his life. Does that make Splash a Buddhist?

The rescue attempt was initiated. Sally grabbed a shovel and started digging Splash an escape route. Phinney started digging right next to her. I am not making this up. Together, they managed to pull Splash out from under the deck, depriving many spiders of a good meal.

This story illustrates an important point about Sally as a part of our family. A few years ago, someone asked Sally what it had been like to live with me for over twenty years. I overheard her say, "It has been interesting." Not wonderful, not terrible, but interesting. I guess that is okay, right?

Moving to Gig Harbor was hard on Zack and Max. They lived in Apple Valley, Minnesota for six years and moved to where they, in effect, started over.

"When we first moved to Gig Harbor, I didn't know anyone, and it was a strange place. Phinney and I had a bond and he slept on my bed every night which gave me comfort. I remember a very specific way I would snuggle with Phinney and Samantha while they were lying on their side. I would lay against them, belly to belly, and stretch their upper front leg over my neck to commune with the dogs. They never seemed to be bothered by this," Max recalled.

I am betting they enjoyed lying next to their younger brother.

A few years later when my niece, Angie Harbin, came to Gig Harbor for Sally and my wedding, she remembers Phinney drinking the boys' soup at the dining room table. Each time they looked away, Phinney's tongue would lap up some more of their soup.

"After we moved to Gig Harbor, Rhonda made me a very special peanut butter and chocolate cake for my birthday. I was very excited, but Phinney snuck in and ate the entire cake!" Max said.

Phinney was a serious dog, never silly, adventurous, and confident.

"Phinney took his job seriously. I wasn't sure what his job was, but he was sure one role was to protect the house. He felt it was his job to make sure everyone in the house, dogs, neighbor dogs, and people did what he thought they were supposed to. He was never pushy or aggressive, but sometimes he made you feel like you disappointed him. Phinney checked the Invisible Fence every day. If it wasn't working because there was snow on the ground or the battery in his collar was dead, off he went to the fire station," Sally recalled.

Phinney never went any farther than the adjacent fire station. Perhaps, he wanted to be like the Dalmatians and ride upon the engine?

Phinney and Sally shared two equine experiences in Gig Harbor. Shortly after Sally came to a party at our house and, fortunately for me and the boys, never went home, Phinney and Splash saw their first horses on a walk with their new mom. According to Sally, Phinney was astounded and fascinated at such a large lifeform. He was less fascinated a few years later when a horse and rider had the audacity to enter his yard without invitation.

Gig Harbor weather is mild and pleasant, especially in the spring, summer, and early fall. Our large front door and French doors in the adjacent room were nearly always open to our veranda which allowed the dogs to independently play "let the dog in, let the dog out." Phinney's self-appointed security duty station was on the veranda, centered at the top of the four steps leading down to the sidewalk. This station afforded a 180-degree view of the lower two-thirds of our property.

Phinney's second equine encounter was different from his first.

"If we were home, Phinney spent his day crouching at the top of the veranda stairs, overseeing his kingdom," Sally recalled.

One cool summer Sunday morning, we heard Phinney furiously barking. Stepping through the open front door onto the veranda, we saw Phinney stretched out, running full speed toward a horse and rider that dared to enter his yard without permission.

The one-thousand-pound horse was having nothing to do with a seventy-five-pound barking black and brown dog. The horse repeatedly arched its back and kicked toward Phinney's head with both hind feet, but Phinney was too fast. The horse reared up on its back feet and the rider slithered off to the side, holding onto the reins. Phinney continued to voice his disapproval.

The rider shouted at Sally. "Call off your dog!"

Sally shouted back, "You're in his yard!"

The rider quietly led the horse through an opening in the hedge surrounding the yard and onto the next lot. Phinney trotted back to the house, tail wagging. He had vanquished the horse!

"I was proud of him when he took the horse and rider down. He was having none of that. The horse did not belong in his yard," Sally stated.

Phinney had a big heart, like all Gordon setters.

Phinney was the lowest maintenance dog I have known. He would gladly warm your feet without invitation for as long as you sat and never attempted to get onto furniture, other than Max's bed. He was this way until the last few weeks of his life.

"Phinney was affectionate with the boys. I remember him lying next to them, letting them hug him. He tolerated affection but didn't seek it out. His disposition was solid, never changing as he aged," Sally noted.

Phinney gladly went on walks, accepted attention or no attention, and accepted almost any and every human and canine that came to our house. He was an enthusiastic eater, eating as fast as a cartoon dog. His ears were long, so if he was offered messy leftovers, we would pull his ears onto his head with a scrunchy. It gave him the appearance of a man bun, which looks best on a Samurai.

* * *

Splash's weather behavior did not change when we moved to Gig Harbor. It frequently rained in western Washington. It was not a tremendous amount compared to Hilo, Hawaii, only thirty-three or thirty-five inches per year but never a downpour like we experienced in Minnesota or Chicago. Rain in western Washington was always a mist, an irritating drizzle.

Splash walked to the open door, stared at the falling rain for a few minutes, turned around, and went back into the house. Once again, he would hold it for more than twelve hours. Splash hated the rain. Splash also abhorred exercise. The few times we attempted to take him on walks around the harbor or hikes up the hill behind our house, Splash stopped, laid down, and would go no farther. He could not be moved. I do not remember Splash ever running.

Before I moved to the Point Defiance Zoo and Aquarium, the Zoo Director, Tom Otten, a close friend said, "You have to come and work at the zoo, and you have to buy my house!"

He wanted a new house so that he could have projects. A few months after we acquired Sally, I reminded him, "I'm buying your house."

"Okay," Tom said.

This was typical of many of the deep conversations Tom and I have had over the years. Tom's wife, Gloria, and Sally were close friends and they believed Tom and I must be having deep conversations about the house sale. Our conversations went like this:

Me: "How much do you want for the house?"

Tom: "I don't know."

Me: "Let's ask your ex-wife, Jill. She's a realtor. She'll know what it is worth."

Tom: "Okay..."

Tom and I continue to have such deep conversations.

The boys and I loved Sally, and she was now stuck! She was on the mortgage. I had entrapped her while she still thought it seemed like a good idea to live with us. Our Gig Harbor home was in Crescent Valley, a semirural area with houses of various sizes and pets of various varieties. Horse trails were present in the cedar forest on the hill behind our house.

Tom and his middle wife, Jill, a wonderful person and great friend, had designed the house known to us as the Otten House to this day. It is a great house. It sits at the top of a slight rise on one and one-third of an acre about a mile and a half from the harbor. A storage shed sits halfway down the grassy slope adjacent to a basketball court and a big grassy yard. It was party central and at least twice a week, friends from the Zoo and their dogs came over for dinner. It was not unusual for ten dogs to be running in and out of the house. At eight-thirty, these parties were over for Sally and me. We frequently went to bed as the party continued at our house or moved down the road fifty yards to Craig Wilcox and Rhonda Wilcox's house. It was a glorious time.

A short three months after we moved into the Otten house, our close friend and co-worker, Traci Belting, suggested we hire Those Darn Accordions who were playing at Zoobilee, the Point Defiance Zoo and Aquarium annual fundraiser, to play at a party at the Otten House. A campy accordion rock band from the San Francisco Bay area, Those Darn

Accordions appeared two years later on the American Music Awards hosted by Drew Carey.

This conversation occurred after I drank either thirteen or seventeen margaritas (they were small, and they were free).

"Let's have them play at a wedding reception!" I said.

Sally said nothing, which was a common response to my brilliant ideas. An answer just short of her more common response was, and continues to be, "Nope."

Within ten minutes, folks congratulated Sally on her engagement. Sally said nothing.

At about twenty minutes in, Tom Otten asked, "What did she say?"

"She hasn't said anything," I replied.

Surrounded by about a dozen people, all of whom had been enjoying margaritas and/or wine, Tom asked Sally, "Are you going to marry him or not?"

"I guess so, but only if he can get Those Darn Accordions to play at the reception," Sally said.

Sally hadn't known me long enough to understand that I was as determined as a raccoon gaining access to a locked dumpster. The raccoon always gets into the locked dumpster. It may have to go to United Rentals and rent a cutting torch or bolt cutters, but it always gets in. Coincidentally, in some circles, I am known as the "Trash Panda," for obvious reasons but that is a story for another day.

Note: This was before the internet so be impressed by my sleuthing, determination (stubbornness?), and problem-solving skills.

I tracked down the band's manager and gave him a call.

"I need the band to play at our wedding reception or I can't get married."

"I am sorry. They are all booked up for months," the manager replied.

"When are they coming back to Seattle?" I asked.

"In three weeks, but I told you, they are all booked up."

"Can you give me the band leader's telephone number? I can't get married unless they can come to our wedding reception."

Wanting to get rid of me as soon as possible, he gave me the band leader's cell phone number.

I called the band leader and explained the dilemma.

"We're booked in Seattle in three weeks, but we are leaving the next day," he told me.

"Okay. What time do you play in Seattle?"

"In the evening," he replied.

"Okay, how about you come to the wedding reception in the afternoon and play for two hours on your way to the gig? We are having a potluck and you can eat and drink margaritas, and I will pay you the same as your gig in Seattle," I said.

I am not sure if I had him at the potluck and margaritas or the pay. I always believe in overkill. Leave nothing to chance. Anything worth doing is worth overdoing.

"Okay!" he said.

Sally was more deeply entrapped. She painfully learned another fun fact: never bet against the Trash Panda and never, never tell him something is not possible! The list of those who have learned this the hard way over the years is long but distinguished. Okay, that is a long, funny story, but what does it have to do with the dogs, you ask?

The wedding reception occurred in the field in front of the Otten House on a very warm, August afternoon. The reception was a potluck, and Phinney and Splash were locked in the garage because we didn't want Phinney counter-surfing. Although there was a big crowd in the yard, everyone loved dogs. They were, at first, going to be in the way because there would be lots of food about and none of them were above stealing a bite. Initially, Phinney, Splash, and their close dog friend, Sammy (a burly and serious shepherd collie), stayed in the garage until most people had eaten their fill. However, it became too warm in the garage and the three dogs were released to join the party. Somehow, Splash managed to get stung on the ventral side of his neck by a bee! His neck swelled up until he looked like a little orange walrus with a black nose. Benadryl didn't help, but fortunately, he had no difficulty breathing.

This time, he was not passive about accepting his fate (Remember before when I asked if that makes him a Buddhist?). Splash began licking his neck as if he were a tamandua (either *Tamandua Mexicana* or *Tamandua tetradactyla*). I could not believe he could bend his head so far forward! How could he do this? As a result of his self-veterinary care, Splash developed cellulitis at the site of the bee sting. Beginning a course of antibiotics, we placed Splash on Prozac as the first phase of Operation Stop the Lick.

Did Splash become lethargic? Did he stop licking his neck? No, he acted exactly as he had without the Prozac. So we placed him on diazepam, better known as Valium. How did he act then? Exactly as he had without the Prozac and the diazepam. Splash had a high tolerance for pharmaceuticals. He previously expressed this when he unwrapped and ate a pound of chocolate-covered coffee beans. Did he get excited? Did he have gastrointestinal issues? No, he acted just like he had always acted. Just like he acted when he was treated with Prozac and diazepam.

The next phase of Operation Stop the Lick was the placement of an Elizabethan collar around his neck. Surely, this would be a success. Walking to the closest doorway, an open set of French doors, Splash pressed the right side of his Elizabethan collar against the right door jam and stood there, channeling his inner Buddhist. We called him. He stood still. We tried to physically move him from the doorway. He appeared to be paralyzed. The door jamb appeared to have the strength of the Death Star's tractor beam.

We left the Elizabethan collar around his neck while he stood at the door, and we offered him water. He stood there. He didn't even bend his flexible, plesiosaur-like neck to try to drink. We held the water up. He stood still, looking straight ahead. He was not only paralyzed, but he couldn't drink. He would stand against the door jamb and die. However, when we walked away, he could still lick his neck, even with the Elizabethan collar. This had to stop, or he was never going to recover. Who was the veterinarian in this relationship?

Sometimes, we see dogs out on walks or at the beach with a small wire cage on their faces, let's call it a muzzle, to prevent aggression. This was my next well-thought solution in Operation Stop the Lick. The muzzle was placed and secured and off we went to work. Returning from work, his neck was wet. He had managed to lick his neck through the small wire mesh at the end of his muzzle! How did he do that?

This inspired the final step in Operation Stop the Lick: placing duct tape inside the end of the wire muzzle. Ventilation holes remained on the top, bottom, and sides of the muzzle, but he could no longer lick through the tiny holes in the terminal part of the muzzle. Splash's neck finally healed, no thanks to him. A golden retriever in a muzzle? Ridiculous!

You may have seen the cartoon image of the many moods of the golden retriever. The cartoon depicts an angry golden retriever, a happy golden retriever, a sad golden retriever, and other moods. The face looks the same in every frame! It's just a simple happy dog face. That was Splash. He didn't want any job and didn't want to be trained. He just wanted to be a happy, friendly, big orange carpet and was never disturbed by anything that happened around him.

Splash was a typical golden retriever in that he liked all dogs and all people except for one person. A newly hired employee and her boyfriend stayed with us at the Otten House for a day or two until they found a place to live. Splash did not trust the boyfriend, never took his eyes off the guy, and intermittently would let out a low growl. This was very not-Splash and not-golden retriever behavior.

Over the next two years, Splash behaved the same way toward this person any time the guy came to the house. We never became aware of the scope of the person's naughtiness, but the individual was subsequently arrested in New York. I am guessing you must be pretty naughty to be arrested in New York. Perhaps Splash, like Saint Lori, could have been a detective? At the very least, Splash was a "narc." If you are too young to understand the meaning of narc, ask Google or your grandparents.

Chapter 10

THE RISE OF PEPPERMANDER

First, where did Bernese Mountain dogs come from and why was the breed developed? The Celtic Helvetii occupied most of Switzerland, first coming in contact — i.e., contact as in destroyed by — with the Roman legions in the first century BC. Accompanying the Romans were large mastiff-like dogs wearing spike collars. The dogs were used to draft, in other words, pull carts or carry packs. They were allegedly used as war dogs. It is my suspicion that these dogs only vaguely resemble today's Bernese Mountain dogs. Although today's Berners can be protective, the enemies of the Romans, greatest risk might be from tripping over Berners laying in the dark (think no need for sentries), choking on or getting Berner hair in their eyes, food, or mouth, or other Berners breaking into their camps during the fighting and eating all the enemy's food.

Regardless, several Swiss breeds descended from the dogs accompanying the Romans including the Saint Bernard and the four breeds collectively known as the sennenhund or cheesemaker's dogs. The four sennenhunde are the Entlebucher Sennenhunde, the Greater Swiss Mountain dog, affectionately referred to as Swissies, the Appenzeller Sennenhunde, and the Bernese Mountain dog, affectionately referred to as the Berner.

All four sennenhund share some conformational and behavior characteristics: including the common tri-coloration seen in several breeds of dogs which is characterized by a basic black background russet stockings, eyebrows, and muzzles, a white "shirt," white blaze, white tail tip and white toes with some individual variations. You can never go wrong with a black shirt, jacket, and/or skirt with a white shirt! Only the Bernese Mountain dogs have long, wavy coats. Entlebucher Mountain dogs are the smallest. They are short-coated and good-natured. They are loving with families but reserved towards strangers. Greater Swiss Mountain dogs are the largest of the breeds. They are short-haired and active, but perhaps more watchful, suspicious, and strong-willed than the other three breeds. The Appenzeller Sennenhunde is medium in size, very active, and needs jobs.

Focusing deeper on the Berner, they are about the size of a collie with a broad chest, short back, straight muscular forelegs, well-developed thighs, and large round feet. They were bred to herd and protect the flock. However, unlike many other herding breeds, Berners slept in the house with the family rather than outside or in the barn. If you asked a Berner if this was true, they would simply say, "Duh!" If you asked them why this was true, they would also answer, "Duh! Just look at us!"

Ranging in height from twenty-three to twenty-seven and a half inches at the shoulder, Berners weigh between seventy and one-hundred and fifteen pounds. There has been a trend toward breeding larger males, often accompanied by the development of hip and joint problems. Berners are affectionate with their families, excellent with children and other dogs, and adaptable and comfortable with strangers. They are moderately good watchdogs and protective of their people and territory. Bernese Mountain dogs are family dogs; they want to be with the family. Berners are not good dogs to leave alone in the backyard for hours, but then, I don't know of any dog breed that does well when left alone in the backyard for hours. I attribute this strong drive in Berners to be part of the family from their heritage. Remember, they lived in the house.

Bred to be draft dogs on small Swiss dairy farms that might not support a larger draft animal, these Berners were clever and transactional. Hooked to carts containing milk or cheese, they pulled the carts into the village to the appropriate outlet. The receiving business might give the Berner a bone, place their empty milk containers in the back of the cart, and the Berner would return home without a human escort. I suspect if the receiving business did not give the Berner something, the Berner stood looking at them until they did receive something. I wouldn't have trusted our teenage sons with this level of responsibility. Berners also did some herding, flock, and herd protection.

They were selected as good-natured, multi-purpose dogs that would fit into the household rather than a high-speed, prey-driven breed, such as the Belgian Malinois.

Here is how our good friend, former marine mammal trainer, zoo-keeper, and Berner owner Paul Povey summarized Berners, "Berners are always happy to see you, always in a good mood, [and] always sorry to see you leave. In effect, Berners make better people than people." Berners are also attention magnets. Paul noted, "Walking around the Harbor with our new Berner was an eye-opener. Everyone wanted to talk to them."

It is time to meet our first Berner, Peppermander.

But before that, let's talk a bit about the name "Mander." At the time the lovely Sally moved in with the boys and me, we were without a girl, other than Samantha. Of course, we had left her behind with Susie. There were no girls in the house for even one night, much less an extended period. Twelve-year-old Zack coined Sally, "Sally Mander." As we all subtly, without any discussion, learned that we now lived in a matriarchal society, much like elephants and dolphins, we became the "Manders." Some time ago I asked Sally when she decided she was in charge because I didn't recall being a part of that discussion.

"I quickly decided I was in charge because I could be," Sally said.

That captures the essence of the Honey Badger; now, here is a true story that captures the essence of Peppermander.

The mischievous eighty-five-pound Berner princess darted and dashed around the exterior of the house, evading Sally's reach at every step. Cookies were offered in vain since Pepper knew that Sally was trying to pull a fast one by locking her up so she could go somewhere fun without her! It was simply not happening! Alas, she was too trusting.

Sally opened the sliding door to her silver Dodge Caravan, the Badger Mobile. The Death Star's tractor beam could not pull Pepper forward any stronger! Resistance was futile! She was going for a ride! It was too late in the day to go for a run on the Sacramento River trail since the other girls were not leashed up in the van, and Sally was not wearing the correct suit for a run. Just maybe, we were meeting Molly and Dad for lunch at In-N-Out?

Pepper raced to the open door and jumped in. She was wagging her tail, smiling, and panting! But wait! *What the Hell?* Pepper thought. She had been duped! Sally reached in, attached a leash to Pepper's purple collar, and led her into the house. *You broom rider!* Pepper thought almost out loud. *Don't you know who I am? Nobody puts Pepper in the house or anywhere else she doesn't want to be. This is some bullshit!* Pepper leaned toward the profane and cursed like a sailor. I don't know where she got that from. Really, I do know where she got that and it wasn't from Sally.

Joy. Joy was the one word that captured the essence of how Pepper lived from the moment that the twelve-pound, ten-week-old, fuzzball with a pixie face and impish sense of humor took control of our home populated by me, my lovely wife, Sally, Phinney, Splash, and our two-footed sons, fourteen-year-old Zack, and eleven-year-old Max.

The little fuzzy whirlwind took control of our household until the day — eight years and four months later — she transitioned to another plane, leaving a Grand-Canyon-sized hole in our hearts.

"Pepper had a commanding attitude. She arrived knowing she was the Queen, the head princess, [and was] in command of the household.

She enjoyed being in charge of the other dogs. From the very start, she could be seen strutting around the house with her tail up," Sally noted.

"Pepper was [a] queen dog. She did whatever she wanted, and everyone let her," Zack noted.

Our dear friend, Becky Wilson remembered, "Pepper was the prettiest of all the dogs. She was the matriarch, the grownup, [and] the most sophisticated. When she was at the office at the Turtle Bay Exploration Park or Turtle Town, she took her job seriously. Pepper was not a push pig. Not that there is anything wrong with being a push pig, Molly," Dr. Zack said.

"Just like Annie who followed, Pepper was [a] queen bee, always pushing the other dogs out of the way. Rhonda Wilcox, Gloria Otten, and I came to your house to sit in the hot tub and drink wine with Sally. Pepper came out and hung out on the deck with the girls but wouldn't let the other dogs come out. Pepper said this was grown-up time," Traci recalled.

Gabriel, ex-Army Ranger, and our semi-son summarized Pepper this way, "Pepper was magnificent, the ruler of the pack. While Pepper did not rule with an iron fist, it was clear that things in the pack ran solely according to her will. She was beautiful, stunning. Her facial expressions were many. If I annoyed one of her packmates either intentionally or unintentionally, Pepper took note. While staying with Pepper, I found little ways to annoy some of the dogs. It was my love language, [my way of] letting them know I noticed them but was NOT their mom or dad. I walked with a cane at that time following surgery for a military back injury. Sasha softly growled when I gently touched her with my cane. If Pepper observed the incident, she sighed, stood up, walked over, and investigated the growling. Once she saw what was happening, she would look at me and lay back down. Pepper always monitored her pack."

You might ask, how did a Bernese Mountain dog come to run our household? Thinking back, you might remember Zachary's dog, Splash, and Rumor, Max's ill-fated greyhound. Max still wanted to pick his dog breed. What kind of dog did Max want? A rottweiler! Rottweilers are fine dogs. They are great pets and intelligent, but realistically speaking, they were not the best dogs for Max since he lived upstairs and spent summers with his lovely mother, Susie, in Virginia. His second choice? A Bernese Mountain dog. You may remember that a Bernese Mountain dog was one of my early choices for a first dog, but they were not easy to find in the 1970s.

Nearly everything that I do is a project and takes weeks of investigation and analysis before proposing a course of action to my lovely bride. These courses of action need to be well thought out to increase the probability that the response will not simply be, "Nope!" or more frightening, "Do whatever you want."

My skin crawls when I hear this latter expression. It does not represent the end of the discussion. It does not mean, "Yes, you have my permission to proceed." Anyone who has been married more than a minute understands that when a wife says, "Do whatever you want," it means, "Do whatever you want and be ready for the consequences of your foolishness, and it will go into The Book."

If you don't know about "The Book," then you haven't been married. All wives have The Book. All misdeeds and errors are entered without an expiration date. You will be reminded of these misdeeds and errors when you least expect it and are least able to stutter some kind of defense. The best responses to these reminders include: "Yes, dear!" or "You're right dear!" or "It's all my fault dear!" Spoiler alert: acknowledgment does not result in the deletion of those errors and misdeeds from The Book. They are in indelible ink.

* * *

In general, purchasing a Bernese Mountain dog is not easy. Reputable dog breeders are rightly protective of their breed and their dogs. It is important for dogs to be placed into, hopefully, forever homes that will fit their personalities. Remember, I first learned this from Ray and Kay Ruse and my first Gordon setters.

Bernese Mountain dogs are common in certain parts of the United States, including Colorado and the Pacific Northwest; however, finding an available puppy takes time. We participated in several of the Bernese Mountain Dog Club of Seattle's meetings and Elizabeth and Roger Pearson introduced us to Pepper's breeder. We were lucky.

The breeder had an eleven-week-old female who was born on December 20, 1996, in a home along the Rogue River near Grants Pass, Oregon to father CH De-Li's Foregone Conclusion and mother Sundance's Alberta Ambition. Keeping with our family tradition of simple names for our puppies, her name was Sundance's First Peppermander. Her more common household names were Pepper, P Mander, Pepper E. Mander, and Miss Priss; she truly was Miss Priss, a unique combination of a tomboy who was the dirtiest of all at bath time and a princess.

As soon as Pepper arrived as a fuzzy, black, white, and brown fluff ball, it was obvious that she was large, in charge, and expected everyone to know it. Phinney and Splash approached her with their tails wagging! They immediately recognized that she was one of a kind! They loved Pepper until the day Phinney passed and Splash moved out.

"Adopting Pepper seemed to be a turning point for the family. She was the perfect dog, well-tempered, well-behaved, [and] friendly to everyone," Max recalled.

Peppermander crystalized our family. Pepper's white blaze was narrow and her white shirt was symmetrical. Her toes were white with a few black hairs at the border, and she had chestnut leggings and sleeves.

Pepper came to live with us when we were employed by the Point Defiance Zoo and Aquarium. As a puppy, Pepper came to the Zoo every day. She would stay in a crate in the elephant barn office except during breaks or lunch when she was taken for walks. Soon, she was going for many walks because several people came and fetched her on their breaks for short walks in the park.

"She loved going on walks in Point Defiance Park. Even as a puppy, she was sidling up to people, convinced that they all should or did love her," recalled Sally.

Note: Pepper's theme song was "If you think you love me, you better, you better, you bet!"

The elephant barn was, of course, occupied by elephants downstairs. However, they were not where Pepper was. Splat, a very cranky, orange tabby was upstairs in the barn. Splat's mother had a litter of kittens at the elephant barn and Splat remained. His job was to keep mice out of the hay room. His name came from the possibility that he might venture downstairs into the elephant's part of the barn, be stepped on, and splat! He did not.

Cats frequently have a facial expression that implies the question, "Why wasn't I consulted?" The arrival of this fuzzball of a dog, with the audacity to bark at Splat as he sat on the office counter where she could not reach him, was met with an icy stare or a swat.

"Splat was not impressed and did not have a high opinion of Pepper. Anytime Pepper tried to interact with Splat, he stood on the table, hissing and swatting at her. Pepper was shocked that he would not come down and play! After all, didn't he know who she was?" Sally recalled.

Pepper transferred her disdain for Splat to all cats. She did not believe they could be trusted. They did not bark. They did not play. They did not wag their tail. An orange cat lived across the road from us. It belonged to the Johnson family. This cat would spend hours on top of its fence across the road, staring at Pepper. Pepper, confined to her yard by an invisible fence, would stand and bark at the cat's rudeness.

"Pepper hated the Johnson cat. It spent hours sitting on the fence, making faces at her, not appreciating her authority," Sally recounted.

Like all good dog owners, Sally enrolled Pepper in a local dog obedience class. Pepper was a very quick learner and would perform her trained behaviors flawlessly at home if cookies were available for a reward. The group class was a disaster.

"Pepper was compliant during training if she was inclined to do what I asked. She made me, a professional animal trainer, look like a donkey if she wasn't inclined to do what she was asked to do in class," Sally recalled.

Pepper constantly barked at the other dogs during class! She would wag her tail, indicating she just wanted to play. Pepper saw no reason to do what Sally wanted her to do. She just wanted to play!

Pepper did not graduate from puppy class, but it was not due to her disruptive behavior. At about four months of age, she occasionally cried when she ran. Large-breed dogs are subject to a variety of possible joint ailments as they grow. If you imagine all the skeletal changes that occur as a puppy grows from eight pounds to sixty pounds in their first six months of life, it is easy to think of the strain placed on their developing joints.

Pepper visited one of the most respected canine orthopedic surgeons in the Seattle region. The veterinarian only performed a cursory examination. He pressed on her back, took no radiographs, and concluded she had severe hip dysplasia. His recommendation was that she have surgery on both hips and be restricted to a crate for rest and recuperation for two months. Like all of us sometimes, he may have been having an off day.

We were concerned, but this diagnosis didn't ring true. I consulted my trusted friend and veterinary associate, Dr. Holly Reed. She examined Pepper and agreed that this did not seem likely. Pepper was shuttled into our local veterinary practice, Purdy Veterinary Clinic, where she was radiographed by Dr. Bob and his staff. Dr. Bob and I looked at her early puppy radiographs. Her hips were fine. Pepper did not need surgery, but she did not return to obedience class either. She did, however, return for round two with Dr. Bob later.

* * *

When the lovely Sally moved in with us, our furniture was sparse and, well, it was crap. When we moved into the Otten House, we purchased some new furniture including a dining table, benches, chairs, and end tables. A few days after the furniture arrived, Sally and I came home and through the front door. We saw Pepper standing on top of the new dining table!

Sally yelled, "Pepper!"

Pepper's legs spun in place like the road runners, etching deep scratches in the tabletop. An end table sat next to the front door. It was adjacent to the window that looked out over the veranda and front yard. Pepper stood on top of the end table a few days later. She was so excited to see us returning home that she road runnered the end table.

Pepper's later radiographic interaction with Dr. Bob occurred when she was eighteen months of age. We wanted to show Pepper in the AKC All Breed Shows which was the equivalent of doggie beauty contests without makeup; however, there was hairspray to increase her eligibility for high-quality boyfriends.

In addition, her hips needed to be certified free from hip dysplasia by the Orthopedic Foundation for Animals (OFA) to encourage her puppies to inherit sound hips. Pepper was required to skip breakfast on the day of radiography in case she required sedation for optimum positioning for qualifying radiographs. After all, Pepper recognized no authority on earth greater than her own.

I escorted Pepper into the Purdy Veterinary Clinic and handed her off to Dr. Bob.

"Dr. Bob," I said. "She is fasted in case you wish to sedate her for the radiographs."

"That won't be necessary. We are very experienced [at] radiographing Bernese Mountain dogs," Dr. Bob replied.

I sighed quietly, much like I sighed years later when the veterinary clinic in Winnipeg told me that they could perform an upper gastrointestinal series of radiographs without sedation on a Bernese Mountain dog named Annie requiring that she swallow barium for the procedure.

Dr. Bob came back and handed Pepper's leash back to me. She wore a great big smile and vigorously wagged her tail! Dr. Bob was covered with sweat. His tie was loose. The top button of his shirt was missing. Her hip radiographs were perfect. Of course, they were perfect. Pepper was perfect, and she would be the first one to admit it. Dr. Bob had been Peppermandered!

Chapter 11

LEOPARDS IN THE HOUSE?

Unlike Peppermander, Phinney was largely indifferent to cats. I mentioned the big orange cat that sat on top of the Johnson's wooden fence tormenting Pepper. This cat didn't really trouble Phinney nor did random cats that he might encounter. However, he was very fond of one cat in particular. That cat was a clouded leopard.

For many years, zoologists believed there was a single species of clouded leopard — the smallest and most arboreal of the large cats, weighing between twenty-six and fifty-five pounds. Two decades ago, zoologists split clouded leopards into two behaviorally similar species: the clouded leopard (*Neofelis nebulosa*) and the Sunda clouded leopard (*Neofelis diardi*). Zoologists are fond of changing animal classifications. There is no evidence that animals care.

Clouded leopards are amazing. They are solitary carnivores, principally arboreal, and hunt small mammals, birds, and reptiles. They are the only cats in the world that run along the top or hang upside down from branches. They use their long bushy tails for balance, and they climb down trees headfirst. What's even more interesting is their canine teeth are the same length as those of a tiger, although tigers are ten times the size of clouded leopards. They are an old species, according to paleozoologists, and are one of the first felids to diverge from the original feline ancestral species.

Combined, the two species of clouded leopards may number only 10,000 animals in the wild. Folks with limited understanding of conservation might think, *well, that's a lot!*

It isn't. Their populations are fragmented in areas with some of the largest human population explosions on earth, some of the most severe abject poverty, and areas that are highly vulnerable to the effects of climate change and deforestation. Additionally, when populations are small, a single novel disease can drive the species to extinction. Not to mention, they continue to be subjected to continual illegal hunting for the fur trade.

The fragility of the clouded leopard's future means every clouded leopard living within the protection of zoological facilities is genetically valuable. Introducing male and female leopards is fraught with danger. Males often attack females which often leads to female fatalities. As a result, a common strategy is introducing the males and females when they are young to reduce aggression and encourage female survival.

* * *

Sally and I were employed at the Point Defiance Zoo and Aquarium and the Zoo was interested in obtaining a six-week-old male clouded leopard cub. Raja was born at a small California endangered species breeding facility to a first-time mother. Like many first-time felid mothers, Raja's mother did not properly care for Raja. He required hand-rearing. It was complicated by ocular abnormalities that led to the development of cataracts in both eyes, necessitating the installation of medicated drops into both eyes every four hours prior to and following surgery to remove his cataracts.

Raja stayed in the veterinary office at the Zoo during the workday which I shared with Dr. Holly. Karen Povey, our lead on the development of interpretive animal programming, and my lovely wife, Sally, cared for Raja during the day, but he came home with us at night for many months.

Having Raja in the house was not like having a domestic cat in the house. He was wild! He roamed the house, cohabitating with Phinney, Splash, and Pepper. Raja was not a cat! He was a leopard. He would hide around corners and on top of furniture. He would approach the dogs and humans with uncanny stealth, leaping upon his selected victim with great enthusiasm and silently appearing behind you in the shower.

Phinney and Splash scurried off, but not Pepper. Pepper, remember, ran the pack. She corralled Raja, holding him gently against the carpet with one foot, and smiled. After all, he was just a cat.

Traci remembers Pepper and Raja's relationship. "The clouded leopards ran by, running sideways on the couch, followed by Pepper who jumped up, landed on your laptop, and broke the screen," she recalled.

Pepper was sometimes an expensive dog.

* * *

PEPPER PLAYING WITH RAJA, THE CLOUDED LEOPARD CUB.

A female clouded leopard cub, Josie, was born at the Cleveland Zoo, and a breeding loan was arranged to bring Josie to the Point Defiance Zoo and Aquarium to pair with Raja. Traveling to Cleveland, I brought Josie home in a small pet carrier that fit under the seat in front of me on the aircraft on Halloween, 1997. Other passengers were unaware that a ten-pound leopard was on board.

Once I arrived home, I set Josie's small kennel on top of the dining room table. Phinney came in, pressed his nose against the kennel wire, and furiously wagged his tail!

"When Raja was in the house, Phinney didn't care about him. He was smitten with Josie from the time she came through the front door," Sally stated.

Over the next few months Josie spent with us, Phinney remained infatuated. Each night when the Josie-containing VariKennel returned home from the Zoo, Phinney followed us closely into the house with his tail wagging wildly. Josie was home! Occasionally, Josie ambushed Phinney. She would leap from the ground, landing on his flank, digging in her claws from all four feet.

A Gordon setter running with his tail wagging while a clouded leopard cub was velcroed to his side…. Well, you just can't make that stuff up!

PHINNEY, EVER INFATUATED WITH JOSIE THE CLOUDED LEOPARD.

Chapter 12

MOLLY THE JEDI MASTER

No matter how many animals and people leave our lives on celestial journeys, some leave larger holes in our hearts. Such folks are hard to talk about, and it's hard to think about the loss. We always encourage each other by saying things like, "Don't be sad that I am gone. Be happy for the good times we have had together," which my friend Jim Antrim repeatedly told me as he was dying from cancer. It was aspirational but not completely achievable for most of us, including me and his daughter, Larne. Sometimes, there is just a hole in your heart or soul the size of the Marianas Trench, and it's a hole that can never quite be filled. Other people and animals can join our path on our life's journey. They can help us create new memories and provide love, but the holes remain for a lifetime.

Mollymander, the Jedi Master, was one of the two smallest Bernese Mountain dogs who made larger-than-life impacts with which I have been blessed. Her protégé and padawan, Anniecan Skywalker, was the other smallest Bernese Mountain dog who made a larger-than-life impact in our lives. Her story will be written in a future book.

Molly and Annie's time in our family spanned over two decades. They both chose me as their primary responsibility and didn't believe that I was safe or capable if they were not by my side. There is considerable evidence that they were correct.

When we decided to add a second Bernese Mountain dog girl to our household, we searched for the highest quality source that we could find. Research suggested DeerPark Bernese Mountain Dogs, founded by Denise Dean and Patrick Hatch, was likely the right fit.

After sending a letter of interest to Denise, I awaited her call. This was before email and text communication were common means of communication. I didn't have to wait long. Denise is incredibly bright, knowledgeable, experienced, and perceptive. She has served as the Bernese Mountain dog representative to the American Kennel Club and serves as a judge for over two hundred breeds at dog shows domestically and internationally. When we first met, she bred Bernese Mountain dogs, occasional Old English sheepdogs, three of which supervised the Berners, and occasional Portuguese water dogs (think the first dog during the Obama administration). Unlike many dog breeders, Denise produced only a few puppies per year and her dogs lived in the house, as Bernese Mountain dogs should. Denise operates a dog grooming business to help support her canine habit and lives on a beautiful, fenced property not too far from the Grand Canyon.

Denise called me one evening on our house phone. We still had a house phone in 1999. Can you imagine?

"I understand you are interested in acquiring a female Bernese Mountain dog from me. Why?" she asked.

Did I mention that Denise is a no-nonsense person? She doesn't waste words and if you have soft feelings, don't ask her a question.

"We have a female Bernese Mountain dog, Peppermander, and would like to have a second to augment our family."

"Are you interested in showing the puppy? Do you think you can make money doing so?" she asked.

"Showing the puppy would be fine, but we never want to be dog breeders. We just love the breed and want her as our own," I replied.

"In case it doesn't work out for you, I want her back! What personality are you looking for?"

"I like strong, assertive, self-confident girls, just like my wives!"

I think that my comfort with strong, assertive females goes back to my relationship with my grandmothers. Both were independent, feisty, assertive, and way ahead of their time. Each had worked in the 1940s and 1950s, not just during WWII. Unfortunately, this assertiveness was not passed on to my darling mother or my little sister; however, it has been present in all my wives and many of my dogs.

Denise and I spoke for two hours. We touched upon the philosophy of animal health, philosophy of life, family, politics, and anything you might think of. Nearly all our thoughts matched up. You see, although I am a veterinarian, I am really an animal person who just happened to go to veterinary school.

At the end of our conversation, Denise said, "You know, you aren't bad for a veterinarian! How soon do you want your puppy?"

That may be the most appreciated compliment I have ever received.

"We are not in a big hurry. We are willing to wait until you have a girl with the right personality."

Grandma Denise has never failed us. She knows what we need and knows what fits our household. Our faux daughter, Wendell, and her husband, Chris, agree. Grandma Denise always knows what Chris and Wendy need as well.

A puppy was born on May 22, 1999, that Grandma Denise believed would meet our needs. Her dad's name was Deerpark Making the Grade and her mom's name was Deerpark What's New. Keeping with our simplified dog naming, the puppy was named Deerpark Mollymander. Close friends called her Molly or Molly Marie and her closest friends simply called her Mol Mol. Molly's white blaze was wider than Pepper's but narrower than the puppies that came later. Her white shirt was more conservative than Pepper's. It was in the shape of a white cross across her chest and a white ascot upon her neck. Molly's feet were a perfect white and she worked hard to lick them clean. Clean paws were important to Molly.

"Would you mind taking a Portuguese water dog pup back to Seattle to its new owner?" Grandma Denise asked.

"Of course not! It will be good company for Molly when she is away from her litter for the first time."

We made plans to bring little Mollymander home. We planned to fly from Seattle to Phoenix, Arizona, and stay overnight with our good friends Dr. Sharmie Johnson, a veterinarian, and her husband, Dr. Warren Johnson, a pediatrician. Sharmie and Warren have two of the biggest hearts on the planet. At any one time, they have between one and four hundred rescue animals of all kinds at their house. They rise at 0400 to take care of the animals and take care of them again at the end of their long days. Sharmie, formerly a Miss Yuma, Arizona, is the veterinarian at the World Wildlife Zoo in Peoria, Arizona. Sharmie planned to drive us to and from Grandma Denise's so we would stay overnight and then fly home.

The two-hour-plus drive to Parks, Arizona from Peoria is beautiful. Starting at the low desert, the road winds through low hills covered with brush and cactus. It then goes past Sedona into the mountains near Prescott and onto Parks which is seventy miles to the east of the Grand Canyon and high on the plain. arriving at Grandma Denise's, mountains could be seen in all directions. Sharmie drove, I sat in the front seat to catch up with Sharmy and Sally sat in the back seat. Sharmie and I always have a lot to talk about.

It was puppy pick-up day at Grandma Denise's. Nearly all the owners of puppies in this litter arrived on the same day. Grandma Denise and her husband, Pat, lived in a metal building with all the dogs during the construction of their beautiful custom home. Dogs were everywhere — Bernese Mountain dogs, three Old English Sheepdogs who appeared to be acting as supervisors of the chaos, a Portuguese water dog, and the water dog puppy.

We met Molly. Often, we use the expression "exceeded our expectations," but Molly didn't exceed our expectations, she exceeded our expectations by light years! She was self-confident and assertive. She threw the other puppies that were twice her size onto their sides and backs. Well, at least she did during the very brief interludes when Sally allowed her to be on the ground. I have never seen Sally happier.

After completing our business with Denise, we loaded little Molly into the back seat with Sally. Dr. Sharmie and I chatted away.

Eventually, Sally said, "I just saw a sign for New Mexico. It seems we have been driving longer than it took for us to get to Grandma Denise's. Are you sure we are going the right way?"

Of course, Sharmie and I were not sure! Paying attention to where one was going while engaging in meaningful conversations was neither one of our strong suits. Sally was correct. We had driven over an hour in the wrong direction. We were driving away from Peoria, heading toward New Mexico. Neither Sally nor Molly was impressed with our navigational skills. It was another reason why I didn't make it into the astronaut program, although I made it through their first cut.

Despite Sharmie and my best efforts, we arrived at the Johnson's house in Peoria.

"It was very hot in Peoria when we picked Molly up. She lay under the patio misters in a puddle, intrigued by Sharmie's splashing tortoise. Her first night away from her mother and littermates was spent at Dr. Sharmie's in her VariKennel. Our thinking that the Portuguese water dog puppy that shared her VariKennel would calm her was off track. She and the water dog puppy sang the 'puppy princess and puppy prince blues' as a duet all night long," Sally recalled.

Once we were dropped off at the airport, my lovely bride and I were booked on separate Alaska Airlines flights because only one dog could travel under the seat in front of the passenger on each flight. Prior to Sally's flight, she parked Molly and me on the terminal floor against the wall. Babies and puppies are the ultimate in chick magnets! Why don't all guys know this? Returning from the bathroom, innumerable young women surrounded Molly and me. They weren't there to see me. They were there to cuddle the puppy, the puppy that looked like a tricolor stuffie.

Molly had class from the moment we picked her up. I unzipped her soft puppy-carrying bag on the aircraft and her puppy head gently fell onto the carpet outside the bag. She quietly slept the entire flight home. Her all-night duet with the water dog seemed to have tired her out. Quite the singer, Molly continued singing the puppy princess blues the first week in her new home. If she was not singing, she was hurling her little body against the kennel door.

Pepper was just over a year old, sharing the household with Phinney and Splash when Molly arrived on a Sunday afternoon to much fanfare. Guests for her arrival included Dr. Holly Reed, Dr. Shannon Donahoe — who has gone on to become a highly competent, well-known veterinary pathologist —, other animal keepers from the Point Defiance Zoo and Aquarium, and Nicholas, the tri-colored Shetland sheepdog.

Everyone wanted to cuddle the little seven-pound ball of fluff named Molly Mander. Everyone, that is, except Nicholas and Pepper. Molly was used to being around a lot of big dogs, such as Bernese Mountain dogs and old English sheepdogs. I am not sure if there are any young English sheepdogs or middle-aged English sheepdogs; apparently, they are all "old." Alternatively, maybe there are "new" English sheepdogs. In any case, Molly approached Nick and he nipped her on the nose. She cried! Pepper, who had been circling the chaos at some distance since she was for some unknown reason not her usual center of attention, was having none of this. The puppy might be invisible, but she was now under her protection. Pepper rushed up to Nick, planted her front feet, lowered her head, and barked in Nick's face. Nick was placed in an exercise run on timeout for the rest of the afternoon.

* * *

Molly adored and practically worshiped Pepper. Of course, she made a few efforts to nurse which were met with rejection, but for the first week, Molly was often invisible to Pepper. Molly could approach Pepper, lick her face, and lie down next to Pepper, and it was as if Molly was not even there. She became visible quickly, however, and they became fast friends for life.

As her predecessor Pepper had done, Molly spent her days in the Point Defiance Zoo and Aquarium elephant barn. She was in her crate while the keepers worked and out of her crate on walks in Point Defiance Park during the keepers' breaks and lunches. She ran through the Park on her leash, running the same path each day, ducking under a root that stretched six inches above a path, and stopping to chew on a different, very special root during each walk. She was known as "Darth Molly" during these early weeks due to her "sharkiness." Everyone in the elephant crew looked as if they had stuck their arms into a barrel of mongoose! She also didn't want to be kissed on the head or, worse yet, have someone blow in her face. Both events were met with growling. This behavior endured her entire life.

Molly accompanied us to monthly Bernese Mountain Dog of Greater Seattle club meetings. "Molly loved going to the Bernese Mountain dog club meetings and [visiting] with everyone," Sally recalled.

Molly was a feisty puppy and gave no other puppies any quarter. Puppies twice her size rapidly found themselves pinned to the ground by the smaller Molly. She won a Halloween decoration at one of the meetings. Dogs of all ages were competing. A hot dog was placed at the bottom of a galvanized wash tub under eight inches of water. Some of the adults tried to grab the hot dog by submerging their faces. They failed. Molly approached the tub, looked at the hot dog, and hit the water with one of her forepaws. The hot dog bounced to the top of the water. Molly snatched the hotdog and ate it to a round of applause. She was a Jedi.

Molly displayed a puppy behavior when she was most excited that we have not seen before or since: the growly run. Growly runs might be executed on the grass or in the house but were always circular and to the left, much like the Indianapolis 500. Sally, Pepper, and I were at the hub of the pattern, laughing. Stretched low to the ground, Molly kept her left eye on the hub, growling as she ran. It was impossible not to laugh. Unfortunately, the performance of the growly run was unpredictable and there is no digital record.

Molly displayed another Molly-specific locomotion pattern through-out her life — the rocking horse. When she noticed one of her favorite people, she would proceed toward the person with a gentle rocking pattern. She was too cute for words.

Molly retained her singing voice as she entered her teen months transitioning to "the breakfast song" which was accompanied by the "breakfast dance." The young girl awoke famished. As soon as our eyes opened, before we started to rise, Molly would run to the kitchen, jump up on her back legs, twist her upper body to the right, and bark. This song and dance routine continued until she had our attention and her breakfast. Madonna would have been proud to have Molly as one of her backup dancers. By two years of age, Molly had become a hard-core bed sleeper and put her dance career aside.

Pepper was the head princess, and Molly was her Regent. Devoted sisters, they were never happier than when they were together. They went everywhere together. Unlike many female dogs that cohabitate, they never jockeyed for position.

MOLLY AND PEPPER, DEVOTED FRIENDS FOR LIFE.

"One of my favorite photographs of all time is Molly and Pepper chewing bones side by side down in the grassy field," Sally remembered.

Molly was the queen of bone chewing. Our girls receive short pieces of raw tibias and fibulas to strengthen their jaws and clean their teeth once per week. As a result, dental cleanings have never been required for any of our dogs. They do wear their incisors down a bit, but they never build up tartar. Note: the bones need to be raw. Cooked bones splinter. Some veterinarians might think providing dogs with raw bones is a bad idea! They might break their teeth! However, none of our dogs have broken teeth and none of our dogs have ever needed a dental procedure. Dogs may also die from endocarditis from bacteria seeded from dental disease or they may die during anesthesia during dental cleaning. No one cleans the teeth of wild wolves and coyotes.

Our girls have demonstrated different levels of interest in bone chewing. Some, like Sadie, who you will meet in Annie's book, only chew for a few minutes. Molly, on the other hand, chewed bones for hours, sucking the marrow from the inside. In fact, upon our return home after bone day, Molly had collected all the bones and placed them within one foot of her muzzle.

Molly grew up to be "Hot Rod Molly." We toyed with the idea of showing Molly so that she could have a high-quality boyfriend and produce puppies. We asked Pepper's two professional handlers, Uncle John and Uncle Mike, to evaluate her at one of Pepper's shows.

"Mike and John, the professional handlers, said they could finish her, but it would take years," Sally said.

She wasn't destined for dog shows as her hind quarters were a couple of inches higher than her front quarters.

Max noted the second reason she was known as Hot Rod Molly. "Molly was scrappy. Looking at her slightly droopy eyes, you might think they signaled a lack of intelligence, but behind the eyes, Molly knew exactly what you were thinking," Max recalled.

She was a Jedi Master as you will see.

Chapter 13

THE ROYAL TRIXENS

We wanted Pepper to have high-quality puppies. Showing Peppermander to a championship might increase the probability of higher quality puppies through access to better boyfriends. If you have not been to an American Kennel Club dog show, they are interesting. Dogs compete within their breed and are judged according to their compliance with the AKC breed standard in AKC All Breed shows. The prudent way for a dog to qualify for a quality breeding partner — remember, I am talking about dogs at present — is to show your dog in AKC multibreed shows to earn their championship. This takes a lot of work, involving travel, time, and expense.

In our minds, showing Peppermander to her championship would be more efficient and likely, less expensive, if we engaged the services of a professional handler. That was what we decided to do. His name was Uncle Mike and he principally showed Great Pyrenees and Bernese Mountain dogs. Pepper loved Uncle Mike, and he loved Pepper. She showed brilliantly for him and was, usually, in the best shape of any of the Berners with whom she competed. After all, she walked Gig Harbor between six and eight miles every morning with me. She settled on six. How did she let me know this was the correct distance? Because she wouldn't leave the house anymore the morning after one of our eight-mile walks. She frequently had extra walks in the middle of the night, often at midnight or one in the morning, when I couldn't sleep because my brain was squirming like a toad over some issue at work.

Peppermander had a short show career, finishing her championship quickly. She premiered on November 21, 1998, at a show in Monroe, Washington. It was sponsored by the Whidbey Island Kennel Club. Pepper completed her championship at her last show in Centralia, Washington in March 1999. Pepper was very popular with the judges; she was very flirty and very showy.

However, she was consistently very unpopular with the other female Berners in her class. It was never clear what she said to them, but uniformly the female next to her would bark or growl at Pepper. Pepper always took the high road and didn't respond which was one more factor in her favor.

Our suspicion was Pepper might be saying, "Your suit looks a little tight to me! Or it's a pity you just blew your coat." More likely, she said something like, "You can show against me if you like. It's your funeral!"

Did Pepper like dog shows? She loved dog shows. Her tail wagged and she panted and laughed immediately upon entering whatever fairgrounds the show was held. She was happy to see Uncle Mike and was happy to see a male Berner named Guido that Uncle Mike also showed. You're probably thinking, *maybe she was just excited there were dogs and people around*. Pepper watched dog shows on television. Okay, lots of dogs might do that. Pepper watched the dogs compete, but when a commercial came on, she put her head down and closed her eyes. Commercial over? Pepper was wide awake with her head up. Thinking back upon this, my dad watched a lot of sporting events the same way...

After sorting through several of Grandma Denise's recommendations for possible Pepper boyfriends, we settled on sending Pepper to Dan and

Celia Cuellar's Sunshine Bernese Mountain Dogs in Redding, California. It was where Pepper continued to express her Pepperiness, not to the delight of Celia. Pepper preferred to associate with men. Like a cute little human girl, she was able to wrap men around her little paw. She wasn't unkind to women, but often regarded Sally, and apparently Celia, as kitchen help. Remember the description of Sally putting Pepper in the van in order to lock her up?

Celia was not fond of Pepper. Pepper was not fond of Celia. Pepper was fond of Dan. Dan was fond of Pepper.

Pepper was not interested in having a boyfriend, especially a boyfriend named CH Rumcay's Quixote V Loewenzahn. She wouldn't stand for her want-to-be boyfriend while she was in heat! Each time he approached her, she wheeled around, saying, "Are you feeling lucky today? Make my day!" Pepper watched a lot of Clint Eastwood movies. Once again, she wouldn't do anything that she didn't want to do. Celia was losing her patience with Pepper, and she was up against the clock. If Pepper didn't stand for a male the next day, she would be artificially inseminated. Luckily, Pepper finally stood; however, it was at a time of her choosing. After all, she was Peppermander.

Pepper was placed on a return flight back to Seattle following breeding. I suspect Celia and Pepper were happy to see the last of each other. Pepper likely had the last word. Grandma Denise coincidentally was staying overnight with us with one of her adult female Bernese Mountain dogs.

Sally retrieved Pepper from air cargo and opened the door to the van. Pepper jumped in, saw the unknown female, and looked at her with her typical "Who the heck are you?" expression. Pepper wasn't ready to share her queendom with another princess, but she was respectful. After all, it was another princess, not a stupid boy.

First-time motherhood for many species is not always an easy event. Depending upon the mammalian species, various degrees of mothering skills are instinctive while others are learned. Additionally, just like with humans, female mammals display variable levels of enthusiasm in embracing parenting responsibilities.

The point is you never know what to expect. Pepper's pregnancy was confirmed through a serological assay of a hormone called relaxin — no, that is not alcohol consumed by humans — which provided us with an approximate date at which we could expect the delivery of the puppies. I say "approximate" because babies come when they are ready. They don't read handbooks, and they take a variable amount of time to be ready for delivery.

A whelping box was needed, and our colleague, Paul Povey, an elephant keeper at the Point Defiance Zoo and Aquarium, constructed the box. It was fit for a queen, just like Pepper believed she was. Bassett Furniture could not have constructed a more beautiful whelping box. The wood was stained dark and elevated about four inches off the ground. The puppies and Pepper would be confined for their first few weeks by the six-inch-high sides of the whelping box.

Pepper's abdomen began to swell; finally, after what seemed like forever, her mammary glands increased in size, and hours after she began labor, she delivered her first puppy on November 3, 1999. Unfortunately, it was a stillborn male. Bernese Mountain dog puppies are about the size of a guinea pig with round Jack-in-the-Box heads and tricolor markings. Their coats are short and slick at birth, but when they are a few weeks old, their coats fluff out like fuzz. Frizzles form on their head and the back of their neck, identifying them as puppies for the first few months of their life.

The stillbirth was followed by the arrival of two healthy females, Bailey, and Trixie, known throughout their lives as the Royal Trixens.

"When Pepper had the Trixens, I learned that puppies are born in a sack. Who knew?" Max recalled.

"Pepper was a good mom. She loved the Trixens [and] loved the Chili Babies, her second litter. She spent a lot of time with Bailey after Bailey moved to her new home and was always with Trixie," Sally remembered.

The Royal Trixens grew and were constantly visited by zookeepers who had eagerly awaited their arrival. Pepper decided that she could no longer eat like her sister Molly, Uncle Phinney, and Uncle Splash. She needed to be fed by spoon in her whelping box and could not possibly eat her normal diet. She only ate the least expensive canned dog food that we could find. It was called Old Roy's.

I am not sure if carp, catfish, or flies would eat this food, but Pepper ate it with a spoon for the first two weeks of the Trixens' lives.

Molly, now a teenager, was enchanted with the puppies. Standing entranced next to the whelping box, she pushed her nose over the sides of the box near the puppies. She was motionless except for her tail which wagged like windshield wipers in a mid-Western thunderstorm.

Her Pepperness was having none of this. Pepper growled, showed her teeth, and snapped a sixteenth of an inch from Molly's nose. Molly remained in place, not flinching at all. She had simply self-appointed herself as their Aunt Molly as well as Pepper's Regent for life.

Usually, dog names come to me from the ether, from senior dog telepathy, or sudden inspiration; it is not clear. So, you might ask, how did Trixie Lou and Bailey Boo become the Trixens? It happened during Thanksgiving Dinner, days after their birth. Max and Zack were away at Susie's in Virginia, but some of our close friends were over for an early feast. Craig, who worked in the elephant barn with Sally; his wife Rhonda; another female elephant keeper; a younger, attractive, would-be-somebody's-girlfriend; Uncle Mark, a long-term animal keeper friend who had lived a year with the boys and me in Minnesota when we were between female house occupants; and lastly, the recently divorced Dan Belting.

A significant volume of strong margaritas pitchers had been imbibed prior to dinner. Mark and the female elephant keeper were both flirting with the young attractive female seated between them. She was what we call in the military a "high-value target." The situation was becoming gloriously tense. Craig, Dan, Rhonda, Sally, and I listened in silence. We were holding our breath with great anticipation as the tension, the palpable tension, rose between Mark and the female keeper. We eagerly anticipated at least a fistfight or maybe something worse. We were not sure which of the bodybuilder's would win. Mark was larger, but the female was way meaner. At one point, the female elephant keeper addressed the younger, attractive female.

"I don't want to hear about you running around with some little Trixie."

Some little Trixie! That's it. I was inspired. The puppies would be the Trixens, and Trixie Lou, stage name Peppermanders Trixen, would be ours. Although no blows were exchanged, and no furniture was turned over, it remains the best Thanksgiving ever!

SALLY, PEPPER AND THE TRIXENS. SALLY HAS NEVER FELT MORE JOY.

Trixie's sister, Bailey Boo, would move on to her queendom with Paul and Karen Povey, an interpretive program keeper, their two Clydesdales, Cleo, her son, Parker, and two kittens.

"Before we moved to Gig Harbor, Karen and I lived in Vacaville, California, and had been discussing what kind of dog we should get to replace our Golden retriever who had died of a brain tumor. We decided that Bernese Mountain dogs were the best dogs that we might have but put the idea on the back burner because they weren't very available at that time. Karen came up for her interview for an animal care position at the Point Defiance Zoo and Aquarium. She came over to have dinner with you. Sally came in the door, and there was Peppermander, a Bernese Mountain dog! It was actually a factor in our moving up to Gig Harbor. We then felt like we had won the lottery when you gave us Bailey Boo!" Paul recalled.

At least once per week, for the next two years, Bailey and her parents came for visits.

"Every time we brought Bailey and Willow to your house, they ran out of the car like school kids going to the zoo. We were suddenly invisible," Paul noted.

During these visits, in Trixie and Bailey's minds, the other dogs were also invisible. They were sisters first. Their first few moments were spent in ritualized cujoing where they snapped at each other just micrometers apart. They never inflicted any damage, at least upon each other.

One evening, as they cujoed, I passed close to them on my way to the kitchen. My right hand passed too close, way too close to their cujoing.

Looking down, I saw a deep puncture in the fat part of my hand near my thumb. Blood was pouring out. I walked to the sink and vigorously washed the dog slobber from the wound. At least ten people were over, including our friend, Ed, who is the tallest Green Beret I have known. Ed was not concerned. I was not concerned. It was just a scratch! Our dear friend, Traci, noticed. The caregiving force is strong in this one.

"When your hand was bitten while Trixie and Bailey cujoed, no one else noticed that you were injured because, as always, no matter what happens, there is no increase or decrease in emotion in your voice. I was mad because you wouldn't go to the doctor!" Traci exclaimed.

It wasn't as if I lost an eye or a limb…

"If it was one of us, you would make us go to the ER," Traci argued.

"What's your point?" I asked.

"My point is that I am taking you to the ER!" Traci said.

Maybe it was the margaritas or maybe over the decades of my life, I have become better at taking direction from strong women. We went to the ER. Upon our return, the cujofest was over and the Trixens were lying side by side.

* * *

THE ROYAL TRIXENS: TRIXIE LOU (L) AND BAILEY (R).

Trixie and Bailey were similar in build. They were both stout girls that were taller and heavier than Pepper. Bailey's head was slightly finer, with a narrower blaze. Trixie's head was a little blockier with a wide white blaze between her eyes. Each had what appeared to be a six-inch long black "sash" that crossed their wide white shirt beginning at their left shoulder and a shorter black sash crossing from the right. Their feet and muzzles were a perfect white. Trixie's coat was fluffier and plushier while Bailey's coat was smoother, much like her mother's, Pepper's, coat.

Chapter 14

QUEEN OF THE PACK

Guests frequented our home in Gig Harbor, and they often brought their dogs with them. There might be ten or more dogs walking in and out of the house.

"Anytime people came to the house, Pepper controlled the crowd. It was like having a movie star amid the crowd. Pepper loved to be the center of attention and was sure everyone was there to see her," Sally remembered.

However, not all our guests liked being at our house when there were ten or more dogs.

"My mom, Nana, hated animals. When she came to dinner at your house, she would be blown away by the cacophony of running and barking. Normally, Nana would sit and watch the whole thing, but she was pushed completely over the edge when people put their plates down on the floor for the dogs to lick. After the third time she witnessed this, she asked that I not take her to your house anymore. Didn't you wonder why she never came over to your house?" Traci said.

I just thought she was busy…

Sundays and Mondays were our days off. Monday was Cono Monday! All the dogs in residence: Pepper, Molly, Trixie, Phinney, Splash, and later, Mandy, and Abigail would pile into the Mandermobile for a trip to Dairy Queen. The girls crowded the open side window, watching the Dairy Queen princesses making their ice cream cones. Pepper was lactose intolerant, and she knew she was lactose intolerant. She would press her mouth between the front seats so Sally could place her lactaid tablet in her mouth which she would then swallow.

Sometimes, we picked up Bailey and Willow at the Povey house for a trip to Dairy Queen.

"They knew the sound of your car even before they saw you coming. They knew it was ice cream time with Grandma and Grandpa," Paul recalled.

Bailey and Willow could recognize Sally's van at a distance. Even while riding in their vehicle, if Bailey and Willow spotted the Mandermobile, their heads would pop out the open windows and they'd bark and bark to follow us wherever we were going. If we were not organized upon our arrival at the Povey house, they would jump up repeatedly, scratching the sides of the Mandermobile. If you do the math, if we picked up Bailey and Willow on our way to Cono on Monday, then there could be as many as eight dogs in the van. Eight dogs expecting ice cream cones.

But who was Willow?

"We were looking for a second Berner and Elizabeth Pearson had a puppy that had been returned to her because it was allegedly a behavioral problem. Elizabeth thought that we were a great fit since we had animal training experience. Of course, when the puppy came home, we found that she was the sweetest little dog ever. Elizabeth gave us the puppy for free with the caveat that we have her bred and she received a puppy. Later, the puppy developed an inheritable eye problem which made her no longer suitable for breeding, so we won the lotto and received two Bernese Mountain dogs for free," Paul explained.

Willow was named by my dear, departed friend, Dr. Holly Reed. She was one of the two kindest people I have known. I was two years ahead of Holly in veterinary school where we began our friendship. We later worked together for several years at the Point Defiance Zoo and Aquarium.

"Dr. Holly came up with the puppy's name, Willow. Dr. Holly, Karen, me, you, and Sally drove Sally's van down to Olympia to pick up the puppy. Dr. Holly came up with the name which was perfect for Willow who was the perfect little princess," Paul recalled.

Like our girls, Bailey and Willow were spayed. Paul and Karen had been around long enough to know that you don't make money in the animal business unless you operate a little or a lot in the gray zone. My apologies to those who believe otherwise. After all, they had two super-sized hay burners: Parker and Cleo Clydesdale. When Bailey and Willow were spayed, I took the afternoon off to pick them up at the Purdy Veterinary Hospital. Grandpa had to make sure they were all right.

"Bailey and Willow were perfect dogs. They were in dog heaven on our five acres, respected the Invisible Fence, and stayed in the kennel when we were at work. They were fine with Karen and me being in the house and them being outside, but if we were outside, they needed to be with us. I saw the wolf genes come out in Bailey and Willow twice. On the first occasion, Bailey was sitting by our fishpond, [and] in a nanosecond, Bailey gobbled down a little brown bird in the blink of an eye. Bailey and Willow could go outside anytime they wanted. One evening, we heard barking and growling coming from Bailey, Willow, and a mom and teenage raccoon, aka trash pandas, or in Canada trash bandits. They were having a faceoff, like school kids that are acting tough and sort of fighting, going back and forth, but not really fighting. I thought, *girls, you are going to lose this fight.* Suddenly, Willow and Bailey drew on their inner wolves, coming at the two raccoons in a delta formation. The raccoons scurried up a tree, and suddenly, Bailey had a raccoon tail in her mouth and one of the raccoons in the tree had a stump rather than a tail. Willow and Bailey circled the tree, growling for an hour. I was sure the raccoon would bleed out, but in the morning, the raccoons were still there. The raccoons stayed in the tree for two-and-one-half days and were then gone," Paul said.

"What happened to the tail?" I asked.

"Bailey ate the tail," Paul answered.

After we moved to Redding, Bailey and her younger sister, Willow, stayed with us for a few days while their parents were in San Francisco. From the moment they walked into the house, after lots of joyous barking, they acted like that was where they belonged with one exception. When the pack approached Sally for treats, Willow consistently turned around and barked at Sasha, the Giant Schnauzer's face. Her attitude was, *if you're not Berner, you are little people.*

Sally said, "Willow was a little pixie!"

Trixie Lou was never a complainer and lived quietly. She displayed two interesting behaviors. First, she would disappear in our Gig Harbor house. How does a one hundred-and-five-pound Bernese Mountain dog disappear? It would occur to us that we hadn't seen her for half an hour or an hour.

Initially, we searched everywhere and asked the boys if they had seen her. Asking the boys if they had seen anything was futile. Godzilla could have been in their room and unless Godzilla was involved in their personal, super important activity, such as playing a video game, they wouldn't notice. Of course, Godzilla probably wouldn't go into their messy rooms. After all, even monsters have standards for cleanliness and organization. Eventually, we learned to look for her in the small bathroom downstairs. Trixie pushed the door open and walked into the dark bathroom. The door would close behind her. She would wait quietly and patiently for as long as it took until we discovered her! Upon opening the door, Trixie Lou walked out, looking around like nothing had happened.

Trixie Lou's second interesting bathroom behavior occurred in our Gig Harbor home and, later in our Escondido house. It was observed twice after her death as you might read in a later book. Trixie, the world's largest plushy with the softest fur imaginable, repeatedly grabbed the end of the toilet paper roll and ran out the bathroom door, down the hallway, and into the yard. It was for no good reason. Unlike Anniecan, who came later, she didn't chew the toilet paper. She just ran with it and dropped it on the ground.

* * *

At about a year and a half of age, Trixie decided that she should be head princess. After all, she outweighed her mom by at least fifteen pounds. Over the course of a few days, Trixie picked fights with her mother. Dogs prefer to fight with their softer belly on or in the direction of the ground, but not Pepper the Invincible. Pepper's winning strategy was to roll onto her back where she could no longer use her leg strength and proceed to win a fight against anyone foolish enough to believe that there was a possibility that they could dethrone the Head Princess. Trixie did not question Pepper's authority again, but she consistently ranked higher than her half-sisters, Mandy, and Abigail.

"Trixie was always a gentle soul, not pushy, not arrogant, not the 'I am a supreme being' attitude that Pepper had," Sally stated.

* * *

HE LEADERSHIP TEAM: PEPPER, MOLLY, SALLY, AND TRIXIE LOU.

We are often questioned by other walkers about the Berners. The most common question is, "Do they shed?" We smile and take deep breaths to control our laughter. This is very similar to the question concerning what bears might do in the woods.

"Nothing can prepare you for how Berners shed. Suddenly there is dog hair on your ceiling!" Paul summarized.

During my Army deployments, I frequently found Berner hair on my clothing which had been washed multiple times, four months after I left home.

Paul made another interesting observation when he said, "Berners have magic fur. Bailey and Willow spent most of their time outside and looked like mud balls. I didn't want to hose them off, but twenty minutes later, they were clean and shiny on their own!"

We were surprised that plant awns, also known as "stickers," did not stick on their luxurious coats, contrary to Sasha the Giant Schnauzer's coat, which was a sticker magnet.

Chapter 15

THE CHILI BABIES

The Royal Trixens were such high-quality pups that we decided Pepper might have a second and final litter, the Chili Babies. Through the Pacific Northwest Bernese Mountain Dog Club, we befriended Dr. Cindy, a companion animal veterinarian, and her husband, Mark, a wildlife biologist, the owners of two wonderful male Bernese Mountain dogs, Yogi, and a much younger male named Bison.

Dr. Cindy and Mark lived in Washington's Tri-Cities area. Arrangements were made for a date. Early in Pepper's heat, we drove her to Yogi's home. Yogi's stage name was CH Sennenhof Rigi Cox, but we all knew him as "Yogi." He was a fine dog. The date was successful. Dr. Cindy and Mark were to receive a male puppy in exchange for the date, and Pepper returned home to gestate. Her twenty-one-day serological test for the hormone relaxin confirmed her pregnancy.

Again, the whelping box was placed in our bedroom, replacing the dehumidifier that pulled a gallon of water from the moist Washington air every other day. Pepper was restless. Contractions were intermittently visible on her sides. However, after over seven hours, well after Dr. Bob's Purdy Veterinary Clinic closed, no puppies were apparent. We loaded Pepper into the Mandermobile and made our 20-minute, 14-mile drive to the Tacoma Animal Hospital which operated an emergency service. Oxytocin was administered, but there was no progress after an hour. The clinician told us Pepper required an emergency Cesarean section to deliver the puppies.

Three healthy puppies were surgically delivered, but the fourth puppy had blue mucous membranes and the clinician suggested the puppy was unlikely to survive. Unfortunately for us, I had no professional standing at the veterinary clinic and, due to potential liability, I was not allowed in the treatment area to attempt emergency resuscitation measures. I continue to believe that, given a chance, we might have been able to save that fourth male puppy. We waited in the reception area. The three healthy puppies were surrounded by soft towels within a cardboard box, awaiting Pepper's recovery from anesthesia. Pepper's final litter was called the Chili Babies and included Abigail, Mandy, and Stevie Ray Vaughn Mander. Pepper slowly walked into the reception area. She was a bit unsteady on her feet, her belly shaved from the presurgical preparation, but she was smiling and wagging her tail. The ride home was uneventful. Pepper and the Chili Babies were placed in the whelping box.

THE CHILI BABIES: STEVIE RAY VAUGHN PINECONE, ABIGAIL, AND MANDY MARIE.

History tends to repeat itself, sometimes with amplification. Molly and Trixie were enthralled with the puppies. As in a rerun, each independently approached the whelping box with their noses near the puppies. Each stood granite still with wagging tails. Pepper growled and snapped an eighth of an inch from their noses. Neither moved. Second rerun, you guessed it, Pepper would only eat the cheapest canned dog food available. It was the same movie, just with Trixie as an additional co-star.

The puppies grew and grew. They wrestled in the whelping box as soon as they opened their eyes whenever Pepper left to make sure her Queendom was running smoothly. Soon, they tumbled from the whelping box, making the entire house their playground. Stevie Ray was the largest, Abigail was in the middle, and Mandy was the smallest. Abigail and Stevie Ray wrestled constantly. They jumped, bumped chests, rolled around, held each other's necks, growled, and snapped. They were an even match. Mandy wanted no part of these reindeer games.

She would hover in the background a few feet away. Mandy remained reserved throughout her life.

Pepper treated the Chili Babies differently from the Royal Trixens. She did not want the Chili Babies out of her sight! They played all over and around her. They played all over and around Aunt Molly and Aunt Trixie. The day came for Stevie Ray to move to his new home with Dr. Cindy and Mark. They arrived with Yogi and Bison, both well-known and good friends of Pepper, Molly, and Trixie. Splash and Phinney were indifferent. Berner business was not their business. Off Stevie went, along with a name change to Pinecone.

Surprisingly, Pepper was distraught! She ran back and forth in a panic over the entire one and one-third of an acre, looking for Stevie Ray Pinecone. She continued this for the next day. We had no idea that she would behave like this since she seemed indifferent when Bailey moved into her forever house. Abigail and Mandy remained with us and Pepper for the rest of their lives. We weren't good at the concept that when you breed dogs, you send them all off to other households. Our household now included Phinneypin, Pepper, Molly, Trixie, Abigail, and Mandy. We did not anticipate that Splash might throw in the towel and move out!

* * *

Mandy's stage name was Mandy Marie Vaughn Mander, but her family names were Mandy and Mandy Marie. Abigail's stage name was Abigail Vaughn Mander, but her family names were Abbie and Abbie de Gail. The twin girls, Abigail and Mandy, were very different in appearance and behavior. Abigail was larger, longer-legged. Abigail sported the widest white shirt and a medium blaze that curved slightly toward her left eye. A small spot of white called a Swiss kiss appeared on the back of her neck. Abigail's walk was distinct, her front legs taking short strides. Good-spirited, she seemed to think everything in the world was amusing.

Mandy was smaller and finer-boned. She looked very much like Pepper but thinner. Her blaze was narrow, narrower than that of Pepper's.

A few black spots dotted her muzzle. Her white shirt was fluffy. Mandy was most joyful and intense when running. She was the smallest and fastest of the girls. Her front legs extended almost straight out from her body at the beach and her paws dug into the soft sand, giving her great purchase. She was a rocket!

Mandy was easily intimidated, and she never wanted to wrestle with Stevie Ray Pinecone. Sally called her Mandy Mouse. Mandy had an endearing habit of sitting by you on the couch and leaning back against you until she was completely vertical, just like any other person.

Max summed up the differences in their personalities this way, "Abigail and Mandy were very different from each other. Mandy was reserved [and] dainty. Abigail was silly, goofy, [and] the comedian of the pack."

Hali noted, "Abigail and Mandy were always a pair, always doing their own thing.

Chapter 16

SPLASH HITS THE ROAD

The "retriever" part of Splash's golden retriever name was a misnomer. Apparently, although he read books as a puppy, he never read the part concerning a retriever's job. Splash didn't retrieve... ever.

Pepper, Phinney, and Splash walked down the grassy hill and onto the grass with Sally, who had a tennis ball in her hand. After all, Splash was a golden retriever and retrievers were bred to retrieve. Not Splash, not now, not ever.

Sally threw the ball. Phinney brought it back but didn't want to drop the ball.

It was Pepper's turn. Sally threw the ball. Pepper brought it back. Sally threw the ball again. Pepper brought it back and, again, received a cookie. Sally threw the ball a third time. Pepper stood there as if she was saying, "Stop throwing it, dummy. Two times is my limit."

Splash, the golden retriever, was Sally's great orange hope. She held Phinney back since Pepper had established that she would retrieve only twice. It didn't matter if cookies were available. Splash, the great orange hope? He stood in front of Sally, begging for cookies. Sally threw the ball, and it bounced down the hill. However, Splash sat still at her feet. How many times did Splash retrieve something during his entire life? Exactly zero. Not once.

Splash is the only dog that I have known to move out of his volition, illustrating the one time he took control of his fate. Our oldest son, Zachary, left for Washington State University following his graduation from high school. This left our younger son, Maxwell Benjibuns, at home with Phinney, Splash, Pepper's first daughter Trixie Lou, Molly, Mandy, Abigail, Sally, and me. I worked out of town at least two weekends per month. I was up to five part-time and one full-time job at that time. Sally occasionally traveled with me if I was consulting in the Bahamas, Hawaii, or Hong Kong. Stephanie Rubio, a coworker, good friend, and frequent dinner guest stayed at the house during joint absences to care for the dogs and alert us if 14-year-old Maxwell Benjibuns had been caught in any mischief such as not coming home all night. It happened.

Upon our return from one of these trips, Stephanie carried her belongings to her car, opened the door, and Splash jumped into the car. Surprised, we were unsure of our next step.

I said to Sally, "It looks like Splash is moving out."

Sally said, "Yup!"

Splash returned each week with Stephanie for dinner and visited with Phinney, Pepper, Trixie, Molly, Abigail, Mandy, and us. However, he lived the rest of his life with Stephanie and her husband, James. He is the only dog that I have known who chose to move into a different home and did so. Go figure.

* * *

SPLASH, THE GOLDEN RETRIEVER WHO MOVED OUT WITH HIS DOG SITTER.

Chapter 17

PHINNEY LEAVES THE BUILDING

Phinney was remarkably healthy. He was sedated and under anesthesia only twice in his life. The first time it happened was when I neutered Phinney on my kitchen table in Minnesota. Don't worry, it was between meals and he was very likely cleaner than the boys. The second time I sedated Phinney was to remove subcutaneous cysts in Minnesota. That surgery was also on the kitchen table. He never visited a veterinary clinic. That is amazing.

He had a long life for a large dog. He lived twelve full years raising children, raising Berners, raising clouded leopards, and breaking in two moms. When he gradually slowed down and started losing weight, it was obvious that Phinney had lived large and his job caring for us was coming to an end. Sally and I agreed it was his time. By this time, Splash had moved out to live with his babysitter, but Phinney was surrounded by five female Bernese Mountain dogs. He never participated in their reindeer games, but he seemed to enjoy being part of the pack. The girls frequently became excited when let out from the dog run, running along Phinney's sides and pulling on his long ears.

We saw no reason to take him to a clinic for a final visit.

"Phinney became worn down over time. He was slowing down and much thinner, but he had grown dreadlocks, becoming a Rastafarian setter. Losing Phinney was hard," Max recalled.

We quietly and painlessly released Phinney from this plane at home and loaded his remains into the van with the five Berner girls. The girls showed no interest in Phinney since they knew his spirit no longer occupied the black and brown dog suit in the van. They were ready to go to the Dairy Queen and waited quietly while we dropped Phinney's remains off at the Purdy Veterinary Clinic. Although I have euthanized other people's dogs in their homes, Phinney was the last dog in our family that I thought I would euthanize at home. I just don't have the heart for it.

However, I was sadly wrong about Phinney being the last…but that is a story for a different book.

Chapter 18

MOLLYMANDER BUILDS A MUSEUM

In late 2001, Molly and I moved to Redding, California. Believing this to be a step toward a zoo directorship, I accepted a position as Chief Operating Officer of the multidisciplinary Turtle Bay Exploration Park. I accepted the position with the caveat that Molly would accompany me to the Museum every day. The leadership team expressed some apprehension since no one had made that kind of request, and they had no idea what she would be like. Would she bite someone? Molly acquired her own employee identification card just like everyone else. She wore logo scarves in bold Museum colors, featuring the Museum logo, identifying her as a staff member. She cared about her appearance at work.

"The wooden bridge that connected the Museum to the Gift Store became very hot during the summer, the surface reaching 150 degrees Fahrenheit. I remember Molly needed to wear booties so that she didn't burn her feet. But she hated the booties [so] she would rather have burned her feet. She literally made herself invisible at those times because she didn't want anyone to see her in her boots," Becky Wilson recalled.

* * *

Turtle Bay, known to some of us as Turtle Town, had an expansive vision. The museum included northern California history, art, a beautiful trout aquarium, classrooms, and a café nestled on one side of the Sacramento River. The Calatrava Sundial Bridge spanned the river leading to an arboretum on the other side. Molly came with me because she believed I needed supervision, leaving Sally, Maxwell, and the rest of the pack behind in Gig Harbor.

Maxwell Benjibuns was in his junior year of high school and our plan was for Sally to continue to work at the Point Defiance Zoo and Aquarium while Max completed his junior year. After which Sally, Max, and the pack (minus Molly), were to join us in Redding. It wasn't to be. Sally and I did not like being away from each other or she was tired of cleaning up after Maxwell. She says we hadn't been married long enough for her to enjoy being without me. We decided alternative housing was needed in Gig Harbor for Max so that Sally and the rest of Pepper's pack could join us in Redding. We first stashed Maxwell at our close friend Traci Belting's house, followed by stashing him at his close friend Dane's house. The change was necessitated by Max's creative behavior. He demonstrated he required supervision.

Molly and I moved into a wonderful six-hundred-square-foot home located on twenty-seven acres in Palo Cedro, California. It was adjacent to Cow Creek, a tributary of the Sacramento River. Trees had been cleared, making way for pasture, and we were adopted by Barb and Dean Davis, two members of the Museum Arboretum Board that we referred to as the "Grandparents." Barb, a retired schoolteacher, and Dean, a retired IBM employee, spoiled Molly and me. We were welcomed as family, and they fed us dinner every night. All we needed to do was show up.

Molly did not develop her world-class begging skills or become known as a "push pig" until we lived with Barb and Dean. Molly sat by Barb or Dean as we had dinner, bumping their elbows with her muzzle until they fed her food from their plates. Molly, thereafter, did not restrict her begging to the Davis household.

Securitas officers Jesse and Talbot provided museum security. Molly and my office was on the Museum's second floor which was the same floor as the employee lunchroom. Talbot and Jesse adopted Molly as a Securitas employee, and Talbot's wife made Molly a Securitas scarf that Molly rotated with her Museum and holiday scarves made by Sally. Talbot's wife packed a double lunch each day, half of which he shared with Molly. But that wasn't all. At least seven snack stations were scattered around the Museum all for Molly. Molly didn't eat at home on the days she worked at the Museum.

"Molly was the ultimate push pig!" Becky remembered.

Imagine a dozen American bison (*Bison bison*), crowding around something edible. If Molly showed up, she would push them right out of the way.

* * *

Prior to the formation of the Turtle Bay Exploration Park Board of Directors, numerous specialized interest groups operated in Redding — a Forestry Board, an Art Board, a Horticulture Board, a Natural History Board, and a History Board, all of which fused at Turtle Bay but each retained board representation. The founding CEO, Judy Salter, an amazing dynamo and self-proclaimed pirate, engaged the support of the McConnell Foundation, the largest non-profit funder in Redding, to help fund the construction of the Museum and the Arboretum. She also used her secret skills to raise funding to construct the beautiful Calatrava Sundial Bridge which spans the Sacramento River uniting the campus. If you haven't seen the Calatrava Sundial Bridge, look up the images online. It is beautiful. At night, it is bright enough to see from space. Judy left a legacy.

Molly was worth her weight in gold at the Museum. The bold vision in a moderate-sized community was challenging. Starting up any new organization is a great challenge. Talented subject matter experts from multiple disciplines and diverse organizations were recruited, but they had never worked together as a team. Operating expenses were higher than the available revenue. Difficult decisions were necessary to match programs and resources. These decisions impacted people's livelihoods and people matter.

This is a recipe for anxiety and Molly was the therapist. She attended senior staff meetings, Board meetings, staff meetings, and contentious meetings with the City of Redding and with the McConnell Foundation, our biggest funder, and she gave people peace. She was a natural-born therapist.

"Molly was always perky, bright, confident, [and] so friendly; she loved everyone," Sally recalled.

It was difficult for anyone to be stressed or sad around Molly.

Molly knew she owned the place. She walked without a leash but usually held one of the ties from her scarf in her mouth as if it were a leash.

"Of all the girls, Molly was the star, [shining] in all ways. She was the Princess and knew that was her right and felt entitled to do and say whatever she wanted. Molly didn't care what anyone thought of her. She did what she wanted to do and when she wanted to do it. Molly could tell that some people weren't nice. She didn't like them back, and knew they were undeserving of her time," Becky recalled.

Molly developed a signature move at Turtle Bay: standing between someone's legs, facing backward, and wagging her bushy tail. If a person didn't pet her long enough or with enough enthusiasm, she laid on their feet. She taught this behavior to Anniecan, her protégé and padawan, who then passed it on to her son, Bunsen, also known as "Pancho."

However, Molly was not the only dog in town with a stake in Turtle Bay. Lee Salter, the head of the McConnell Foundation, owned a feisty border collie named Annie. Annie thought she was the most important dog in Redding and objected to Molly usurping her authority. Lee and Judy invited Sally, Molly, and me to dinner. Molly and Annie skirmished all evening in the backyard which was odd because Molly was gentle, benevolent, and got along with all dogs and cats. The evening ended and

Annie Salter made what she thought was a tactically brilliant move as Molly jumped into the back seat of the PT Cruiser. Annie bit Molly on the butt! The nerve!

Annie Salter was outraged and remained outraged for the next two-and one-half years that Molly worked at Turtle Bay. It might seem that Annie and Molly would not encounter each other. After all, Redding is a community of eighty thousand people. Not so… On more than one occasion, Molly showed up at Trilogy Architects for a morning meeting only to find Annie Salter in the conference room in an earlier meeting. On either side of a glass door, Annie and Molly were immobile, and then it was game on! They would snarl, snap, and slam into the glass door. They obviously had not worked through their differences.

Before the museum opened to the public, Molly ended up with the upper paw. The hallways in the original Turtle Bay offices were lined with boxes of materials that had been printed in anticipation of opening. Office doors opened into the hallway.

As Molly made her morning rounds through the offices, greeting each of her employees, Lee and Annie Salter rounded a corner unannounced. Neither was on a leash. Leashes were for ordinary dogs, and they were not ordinary dogs. Annie's presence in Molly's office compound was not to be allowed! Off Annie ran down the hallway with Molly in angry pursuit, snarling, growling, and knocking boxes in every direction. Office doors were slammed, and people ran for their lives.

Finally, Annie was safely locked behind an office door. It seemed Molly had told her not to come back. Interestingly, Annie Salter had a nearly identical sister, Daisy, who occasionally came to Turtle Town. She would lie under the desk of my administrative assistant, Linda. Molly, Pepper, and Trixie all got along with Daisy. They frequently lay down next to Daisy. Daisy didn't like Annie either. Annie later was kicked in the head by a horse. She lived. The horse didn't like Annie either.

In the company of realtors and before Sally's arrival, Molly and I looked at a rural property on which we would live with Sally, the pack, and Maxwell Benjibuns. Molly and I narrowed the choices down to two possibilities but didn't have the authority to decide on which to make an offer. Sally flew from SeaTac to Redding's airport, which is small, but wonderful. The very best restaurant in town, Chu's, is upstairs in the airport.

Molly and I entered the airport to pick up Sally. Molly wasn't expecting her. It took two seconds for it to sink in. Mom was here! Molly nearly knocked her over. Squealing with delight, she gave Sally a thousand kisses. They were both so happy.

"It was one of the most touching moments of my life," Sally recalled.

Chapter 19

PEPPERMANDER MOVES HER PACK

I visited Gig Harbor only twice before Pepper's pack moved to Redding. It was a day's drive each way. Molly stayed behind with the Grandparents during my second trip, but I brought Pepper back with me. Arriving at the Grandparents' house, Pepper and I parked in front of the little house that Molly and I shared. As I opened the car door, Pepper ran into and around the little house. She was so excited! She smelled her sister Molly! Running in and out and panting with her tail wagging, you could almost hear her shout, "Where's Molly? Where's my baby sister?"

Molly was next door at the Davis house. Pepper jumped up onto the veranda, clearing all four stairs! "Where is my baby sister?"

A joyous reunion accompanied by barking, running, jumping, and tails wagging followed. Thus, began the second chapter in Pepper's life, the second town that she came to own.

Pepper enjoyed the twenty-seven acres on which the Davis family lived. The majority of the acreage was pasture and Pepper explored. She ran through the pasture, smelling where deer and turkeys had walked.

Running through the grandparents' pasture, Pepper saw me on the house veranda. She picked up the pace and ran straight into the swimming pool without hitting her furry brakes. Getting out, she shook herself with no embarrassment. She looked around as if to say, "I meant to do that." Peppermander was never embarrassed. Queens do no wrong.

Our five, count them *five*, Bernese Mountain dogs joined us on five fenced acres complete with hundreds of scruffy gray oak trees. Sally's all-time favorite house sat in the center.

"One of my favorite memories is the girls meeting the UPS or FedEx truck at the gate, getting in the van, and riding to the house, at which they would get out and let the gentleman make their delivery," Sally said.

It is true. The UPS or FedEx drivers opened the gate, drove through, closed the gate, and all the dogs that were home jumped in and rode up to the house where they got out.

"All the girls loved the fenced spacious Redding yard. The weather was such that the door could be open nearly year-round, letting the girls run and run and run," Sally remembered.

Throughout our lives, people sometimes say surprising funny things that they don't mean to be funny. The Sacramento River Trail ran along both sides of the Sacramento River, just north of Turtle Town. Nearly every day, Sally would walk or run as many dogs as were home with her for six miles. At the end of one of our Trail walks, as we walked back to the car, two people approached us from the other direction.

One of the walkers asked me, "What kind of dogs are those?"

"Bernese Mountain dogs."

As we continued to walk to the car I heard, "Who's Bernie?"

* * *

Trixie was the third Berner to spend time at the Turtle Bay Exploration Park. Unlike her mother, Pepper, Trixie was never fired, and she never decided to go in a different direction which is common terminology for, "I got fired!"

"Trixie liked going to work and behaved herself because she was sensitive and didn't want to get in trouble. She got along with everyone.

Trixie was my favorite. She was big [and] poofy, like a big teddy bear. She was always happy, easygoing, went along with whatever was going on, and never got irritated with anyone," Becky recalled.

Trixie had two favorite people at Turtle Town. The first and longest was her Aunt Becky. Becky was the glue that held Turtle Town together, always the objective problem solver. Trixie disappeared upon our arrival at Turtle Town, but she was not locked in the bathroom again! No, Trixie most likely was lying on the carpet in Aunt Becky's office. If not with Aunt Becky, then Trixie could be found in the office of our first of two interim Executive Directors, Ms. Nancy Schultz.

Nancy was as kind a person as you could ever meet. She was inserted into a raucous group of four strong-willed senior managers that kept the institution afloat over the succession of four CEOs. She was gentle, courteous, and in other words, not like us.

A few weeks into her stay she interrupted us and said, "You guys suck! You interrupt each other and talk over each other all the time!"

We had corrupted Nancy and forced her to say we sucked. In any case, Trixie adored Nancy and sat by Nancy as Nancy worked her keyboard, occasionally "helping" by hitting the keyboard with one of her big front paws.

Although supremely confident, Trixie had one phobia at Turtle Town and a single startling experience. In the center of the Museum's main hall was a dead tree. It was stripped of its leaves, and its roots extended down through the glass floor, illustrating that as much of the tree lived underground as above the ground. Trixie would not walk on the glass! The glass floor did not phase Pepper or Molly, but Trixie seemed sure it would break!

Trixie's startling experience involved a stuffed mountain lion (*Puma concolor*) in the Museum conference room. The mountain lion stood in the conference room for weeks during which Trixie had participated in meetings, but she had not noticed its presence against a large glass window facing the main museum hall. Entering the narrow conference room, accompanying the other participants, Trixie came to a dead stop four feet from the mountain lion. Her ears lifted slightly. Standing statue still, she stared at the large cat with a *WTF* look on her face. Slowly, she approached the mountain lion from its left hip. It didn't move! She bumped its hip with her nose. It still didn't move. Concluding that the mountain lion was not a risk to her or any other participants, Trixie returned to lie in the doorway.

The Chili Babies had great joy during the years we lived in Redding. Their acreage was a treasure trove of ground squirrels, occasional jackrabbits, occasional turkeys, and turkey vultures flying overhead creating shadows on the ground. They were all for the chasing. Sometimes, they were joined by Sasha's best friend, Robbie, a Bernese Mountain dog related to Molly. If an intriguing life form or shadow of a life form was spotted, off they would run, barking all the way! The barking did not lead to great success in apprehension, but on at least one occasion, Mandy caught a ground squirrel. The squirrel administered a single nose scratch after which Mandy delivered the classic "vigorously shake the small life form" move which, as usual, ended the squirrel's life. The girls were ecstatic. Mandy paraded with the squirrel in her mouth, but only briefly, as Trixie Lou snatched the squirrel and began her own parade.

World-class Cujoing was a Chili Baby specialty. At irregular intervals throughout the day, Mandy and Abigail could be seen sprinting through the house, sliding on rugs, enthusiastically skirmishing, and snapping and growling as they ran with tails a-wagging. Their lack of accounting for braking distance on non-carpeted floors resulted in occasional sliding or slamming into walls like clumsy base runners. In one case, this necessitated the repair of a six-inch hole in the sheetrock wall shaped like one of their heads.

Like many twins, the Chili Babies were inseparable. They would sit, stand, or lay close to one another. They often shared glances of unspoken communication as twins often share.

"Abigail and Mandy were like stepchildren. They didn't earn the right to do the other stuff the other girls did. They were the babies. They didn't get to go to the office. They were good girls, had each other, and accepted their place in the standings. If either was alone, it probably would have been hard for them," Becky said.

Chapter 20

SASHA JOINS THE PACK

Redding is located north of Chico, California, home of California State University Chico and a succession of minor league baseball teams. The university infused community character which was a revelation to me. I didn't realize how much the presence of a university could change a community and the demographics of its residents. Founded in 1887, California State University, Chico, is California's second oldest university and gives the community a different vibe than communities of the same size without universities.

I continued my consulting work at zoos and aquariums and traveled many weekends to Hawaii (poor me), Chicago, and Tacoma. However, I valued my time at home with Sally and Maxwell Benjibuns. Max's older brother could not say Benjamin at the time of Max's birth, so he called him Benjibuns instead. The name has stuck into Max's adulthood.

Occasionally, we drove south to Chico, had lunch, and stopped to pick up tamales at Tamales Colima, located at 7866 Highway 99 East, Los Molinos, CA. They were spectacular. The restaurant is still there. If you find yourself on Interstate 5 North and see a sign for Highway 99 E, make a turn and have yourself some tamales. You are welcome.

Not looking for an additional canine family member, but looking for doggie excitement, we took a drive down to Chico for an AKC all-breed dog show hosted by the Butte County Kennel Club. We walked through the merchandise and saw the myriad of toys, clothing, leashes, and food dishes meant to capture the interest of people obsessed with their canine companions. This group is large, distinguished, and includes all who participate in all breed shows. We walked by the various rings and saw working breeds, sporting breeds, and dogs of all shapes and colors. At the periphery, what did we see? A Giant Schnauzer pup, no more than fifteen pounds in weight, wearing a purple collar and running in an exercise pen.

Could I walk by and say nothing? Of course not. I can never walk by a dog and ignore it! She was a darling bundle of energy. I asked the owner, "Where did this little Giant Schnauzer come from?" She provided me with the breeder's name and address.

In ancient times, we sometimes communicated with something called a "letter." It involved writing words on paper, folding the paper, placing the paper in the envelope, placing a stamp on the envelope, and placing it in a mailbox. Days later, the intended recipient received the letter in their mailbox, opened the envelope, and read the letter. Imagine that...

This took days and was very personal. Waiting patiently, I received an initial reply with a telephone number and email address. Of course, I initiated further communication, writing about our interest in acquiring a little girl. The breeder wrote back concerning a future litter, followed by months of silence.

As the months went by, my lovely Sally said, "She will never write back. You need to just forget this."

Sometimes, Sally is not encouraging. This never ceases to amaze me because I have so many creative ideas. I lean toward the other end of the spectrum, always believing that things will work out and that I will find a solution. Maybe that is because I confidently make terrible decisions all the time and they always seem to work out…

* * *

Ocean Park is an oceanarium in Hong Kong. For several years, I provided veterinary services to their marine mammal, bird, and fish collection while their regular veterinarians were on vacation. During my final trip to Hong Kong in 2002, after which I nearly died following my return, the breeder sent me an email. She had a female puppy for us, born August 10, 2002, if we remained interested. Of course, we were interested.

The breeder sent us early photos of Sasha and her siblings. She was so stocky. Facing the camera, her back legs were spread wide, her front legs were evenly placed, her head was up, and she was smiling slightly, gruel apparent at the corners of her mouth. In another photo, Sasha cujoed one of her siblings, grabbing it by the skin on her sibling's right shoulder. In another photo, she seemed like a hungry puppy and was standing in her food!

Since I was not yet ill, I made plans to travel to Pennsylvania to pick the puppy up. By the time I arrived back in Redding from Hong Kong, I was too ill to travel for the next several weeks. I lost twenty-six pounds in six weeks and survived on half-strength Gatorade and Milk Duds.

Sally said she would be glad to pick up the puppy. Sally traveled to Pennsylvania and drove through the farmland to the breeder's home at Ingebar Giant Schnauzers. She was introduced separately to Sasha's father, Ch. Gloris Fatum, and Sasha's mother, Ingebar's Isn't She Lovely. Apparently, the two were no longer close or it had been an ephemeral relationship. She was then introduced to the little tank of a dog named Sasha by us! Her legs and fur were short and her coat was a solid black, but she already had her little beard.

Of course, all American Kennel Club registered dogs must have an official name, like a stage name, and then a name by which they are called. Sally and I tend to be less flowery and more basic than most so we named her Ingebar's Sasha Manderpants. We called her Sasha Stickerbritches (as stickers in Redding were constantly tangled in her bristly hair), Inky, and the Inkster. She was Sally's little angel.

The three younger Berners, Trixie, Abigail, and Mandy rudely welcomed Sasha. Mandy, especially, seemed to think that smaller dogs were squeaky toys. She would push them with her nose to try to make them squeak. They pulled her legs, pulled her ears, and pulled her stub of a tail until they made her cry. The older, more regal Berners, Pepper, the head princess, and Molly, the Regent, were kinder.

Sasha could find solace by lying with either Pepper or Molly where she was safe from the marauding horde. Our nearly half-of-a-lifetime wonderful friend, Becky Wilson, and her husband, Phil, frequently had dinner with us in Redding.

"I will never forget when Sasha was a puppy. Sally had placed an oven pan in the dishwater. I came around the corner and Sasha was standing in the dishwasher, holding the pan still with her shoulder against the pan, so she could lick it clean. Sasha was one of the few non-Berners that could have survived in the pack. She thought she was superior to the Berners and prided herself on not slobbering ever. My favorite bumper sticker was the one you had on your car that said, 'My Giant Schnauzer is smarter than your honor student.' She probably was!" Becky said.

I had forgotten that bumper sticker. Was I insensitive?

* * *

Sasha was tightly bonded to Sally.

"Sasha was Sally's dog and was constantly with her," Zack recalled.

"Sasha was my little girl. She was very bright and easy to train," Sally said.

Sasha started her obedience and agility work immediately. Sally constructed an agility course in our yard. The agility course included a tunnel, teeter-totter, weave poles, stay table, A-frame, jump, circle hoop to jump through, and an elevated walkway. All of the girls eagerly participated in all the activities except for Pepper. Pepper chose which activities she participated in.

Sasha was a canine genius. She excelled and loved to learn.

"Find it" was her favorite game. I placed Sasha in a sit-stay in front of the house, walked all the way around the house, hid my glove, and yelled, 'Find it!'" Sally recalled.

Off Sasha went. Without error, she would find the object in seconds.

"Sasha had a very close relationship with Sally. It seemed Sasha conjured up Sally's inner animal trainer in a way that the other dogs didn't. I remember Sasha curling her body against mine. She was clearly much smarter than the Berners and knew she was smarter," Max recalled.

Sasha loved the six-mile trail walk/runs each morning with her five Berner sisters. A former auto bridge was our crossing point closest to town, and a pedestrian bridge was located at the end of the trail closest to Shasta Dam. Sometimes, the girls and Sally ran, and sometimes, they walked. It depended on the weather. The greatest excitement came when an occasional deer stood on the trail like, well, a deer in the headlights. Occasionally, Sally was able to keep the girls from running in chase, although it was not often. However, they couldn't go far since they were strung together. Occasionally, Sally did not let go and the girls might pull her into a tree.

"I came down and spent a week in Redding. I remember going out on a River Trail walk with Sally. All six dogs were harnessed up like Clydesdales, running in front of Sally. We had to go fast and [the] other people on the trail just stopped and stared," our good friend, Traci Belting, recalled.

"Sasha was my favorite. She was so serious. Sasha thought she was surrounded by clowns and stood back and yelled orders at the other girls. One of my favorite Sasha behaviors was when she stood leaning against you with her body comma-shaped. After Sasha drank water, she and her soaking, wet beard would slobber all over you. This was a major leap for me concerning dogs," noted Chris Spaulding.

Sasha took rules and walks very seriously. We always suspected it was her German heritage. An aged yellow line was still present on the asphalt of the former auto bridge. Sasha consistently walked that line, one foot in front of the other. Johnny Cash's "Walk the Line" might have been her theme song.

Sasha had more rules. Horses lived across the road. Sasha's rule was not to trust them. They never made a sound. They just stared at Sasha, and she stared back for long periods. Another of her rules was that bedtime was eight thirty in the evening. She would quietly disappear into the bedroom. If we didn't follow her lead, she reappeared a few minutes later, stared at us, sighed, and returned to the bedroom. This continued every few minutes until we took her direction and went to bed.

Sasha was our self-appointed security chief. Although she was leashed with two Berners, Sasha walked point during trail walks. First out of the van and first into the house was always Sasha. At least once per day, she searched the perimeter of the fence surrounding our property.

"I loved watching Sasha run the perimeter of the five acres in Redding every day, checking the fence line. She was the protector. On one of our walks after we moved south to Escondido, a person standing across the street attracted her attention. She stood between me, the other dogs, and the guy. Her hackles [were] up, [and she] never [took] her eyes off him as she herded everyone to safety," Sally said.

If you are looking for a dog that is a good protector but isn't aggressive and is a good family dog, then Giant Schnauzers are a good choice. But, like most working dogs, they are stubborn and need jobs.

"Sasha always needed a job. She wasn't content to lay around like a Berner," Sally noted.

I feel compelled to say it again. Working dogs need jobs, just like I do. If you don't give them a job, such as obedience work, agility work, therapy work, or regular exercise, they will invent a job of their own and you probably won't like the job that they pick. Sally feels the same way about me.

"Giant Schnauzers also require grooming, every six weeks, so I YouTubed Giant Schnauzer grooming and groomed Sasha myself," Sally said.

* * *

I mentioned Sasha met her best friend in the entire world, Roby, in Redding. Roby's dad, Pete Weaver, was a community college professor, and his mom was a pediatric oncologist, one of the toughest professions on earth.

Roby came to daycare with Sally several times per week. Sasha watched Roby's black BMW roadster come up the driveway to the house. Pete opened the passenger door and stood back. Each time, Sasha would jump into the car and the wrestling began. It would then continue out of the car, followed by running, playing, and more wrestling.

Redding gets warm in the spring and summer, and Roby and Sasha also got warm from their chasing and cujoing. Luckily for them, we had constructed a 3,000-gallon fishpond just outside our patio. Into the pond, they went no longer playing but cooling off.

"What fun that she and Robby had. They were best friends, jumping in the pond and playing," Becky remembers.

SASHA RELAXING FROM THE REDDING HEAT IN HER KOI POND.

Sometimes, Robby stayed for Sasha's birthday parties.

"Sasha's birthday parties were always fun when she wore the leis around her neck," Becky noted.

We were a bad influence on Pete. Eight months of the year, we dined on our covered patio. It was built for us by Tom (the) Lemur to enjoy the pleasantly warm weather. Our close friends, Becky, Phil, and Steve Lester, Turtle Town's Chief Financial Officer, frequently joined us. A pitcher of margaritas, which was considered strong by some people's standards, chips, and salsa always sat on the table.

After finishing his day educating Redding's community college students, poor Pete stopped by to pick up Roby. He planned to cook dinner for the lovely Carol in the evening. However, the lure of the margaritas was too strong for Pete. Two hours later, he was still having a good time and Carol's dinner had not been placed upon the stove.

Sasha was a bed dog. Her first couple of nights, she slept in a crate next to our bed. Well, she didn't really sleep. She sang the Puppy Princess Blues that most of our puppies sang their first few nights. Crawling out of bed, Sally lay next to her crate, petting the little puppy through the wire. Sasha stopped crying. As soon as she was large enough, Sasha came up onto the bed and slept in a little ball at Sally's feet the entire night through until the day before she was no more.

Chapter 21

PEPPERMANDER MOVES HER PACK SOUTH
TO GOD'S COUNTRY

A few years and four CEOs later, it was apparent that my job as Chief Operating Officer was at risk due to inadequate funds. My strong advocacy of the organization, even when it wasn't wanted, and willingness to make difficult, but sometimes unpopular decisions, put my job at risk. The willingness to make tough decisions does not ensure finishing first in a popularity contest.

I attempted to eliminate my job on more than one occasion to balance the budget, but I failed each time. However, I recognized it was just a matter of time before I would receive the proverbial boot. The Museum could not fully afford its grand vision. Rather than wait for the inevitable day when there would not be enough money to pay me, I accepted a position in San Diego.

Although Sally loved her home in Redding more than anywhere else she had lived, we reluctantly left our five acres, the house that Molly and

I found, and our close friends and made the trek to San Diego. We lived with my mother, Grandma Nonie, for a bit before Sally, Molly, and Sasha found our new house in Escondido, California, a few miles from Kit Carson Park. San Diego had advantages. My mother, aunt, niece, and closest friends all lived in San Diego. San Diego has some of the loveliest beaches in California and the sites of my favorite fishing.

Sasha and the girls continued their walks in Kit Carson Park. It was a 285-acre park near the San Diego Zoo Safari Park. The park was named after Kit Carson, the explorer who crossed the Sierras in exploration of California. Kit had a checkered past, leading the military campaign that rounded up 8,000 Navajo and placed them on a reservation. It is unlikely that any First Nation people have named a park after Kit. Paved trails wound through a one-hundred-acre park-like setting with grass and trees. Unpaved trails wound through the one-hundred-and-eighty-five-acre undeveloped area of the park. Cattle had grazed in this area as late as the 1960s. The absence of grazing cattle converted the area from grass to brush. Jackrabbits, occasional coyotes, and other wildlife were often sighted in the brushy, undeveloped part of the park. Every day walks meant seeing the regulars with their dogs and those without dogs.

"I loved it when we went for walks with Sasha in Escondido. If she saw Jerry, who brought her cookies, off she would go!" Becky recalled.

A small pond in the park center provided the opportunity for the pack to lunge slightly toward the ducks before Sally halted their progress.

$$* * *$$

For a time, Molly, sometimes with Pepper, or Trixie, accompanied me to my new position in Old Town, San Diego. Driving down from Escondido at four-thirty in the morning, I exercised at 24-Hour Fitness and whichever girl was with me went for an extended walk around Mission Bay. Sometimes, we ended up at Dog Beach in Ocean Beach after which we headed to the office. Old Town has more character than many places in Southern California. At lunch, Molly, or Molly and Pepper, or Trixie and I walked through Old Town and purchased handmade tortillas from the women who mixed and cooked tortillas by hand by the sidewalk. On many occasions, the girls were described as "bonita." The girls remaining at home walked through Kit Carson Park, went to the dog park on Fiesta Island, and sometimes went to Dog Beach in Coronado, California. Sally worked for a year at the San Diego Zoo, then concluded she would rather be "funemployed."

Trips with Sasha to the beach in Southern California were frequent. Sometimes, these field trips ended at Coronado's dog beach and sometimes, at Mission Bay's Fiesta Island. Sasha was less interested in the ocean and more interested in the ground squirrels found on the other side of the fence on Naval Air Station Coronado's golf course.

Hali Eden, Sally's close friend from the San Diego Zoo, often joined us with her dogs.

"I recall one trip to Coronado dog beach with Sally, Sasha, and my two dogs, Saylor and Sylvie. It must have been a very low tide because Sasha ran around the military fence to chase squirrels. We called her back, but it was a tense moment. The naval squirrels were irresistible to Sasha. Sasha was such a smarty. She had such a strong presence and such a strong bond with Sally," Hali recalled.

We often met our good friends Jim and Jennine Antrim and their dog, Fern, on our outings. Field trips often ended with a trip to McP's, an outdoor restaurant and SEAL team pub in Coronado where the girls shared French fries.

Sasha's favorite trip was to Grandma Nonie's. Sally and I worked at the Chula Vista Nature Center which was renamed the Living Coast Discovery Center. It was located just two miles from Grandma Nonie's. The girls frequently stayed with Grandma Nonie for daycare while we were at work. Nonie enjoyed the company.

The red San Diego Trolley provided Sasha with a highlight when the Mandermobile was forced to stop perpendicular to the tracks to allow the Trolley to safely pass.

Coming and going into and out of the backyard, the Berners entertained themselves through a doggie door. Sasha spent the day with Grandma Nonie, lying on whatever couch was opposite Nonie. Nonie read articles from the *San Diego Union* to Sasha. Nonie was convinced Sasha was a Baptist and a Democrat. They agreed on everything. Sasha barked at any disturbance at either door. Nonie, an older lady living by herself, encouraged this. Sasha loved Nonie and felt responsible for Nonie, and Nonie loved Sasha more than any dog she had ever known.

Chapter 22

THE TAO ACCORDING TO PEPPERMANDER

Many philosophies, especially East Asian philosophies, and religions believe there is a natural order of the universe, often known as Tao or Dao. Philosophers across the ages have described the Tao as difficult to sense since it needs to be experienced through life. I may not have this correct, but, as I have said, "Damn it, I am a doctor, not a philosopher!"

Pepper did not find her Tao challenging. It was obvious and she lived it every day of her life. She eagerly shared her wisdom with any who were smart enough (her words, not mine) to listen. Molly always listened and after Pepper's passing, Molly made sure that I had it straight so I could enlighten others. They will make you think too. If not, Pepper always agreed with comedian Ron White who said, "You can't fix stupid!"

If you're not a Princess, you are little people. Pepper knew she was special, knew she was better than anyone else, even better than other Bernese Mountain dogs, who, according to all Bernese Mountain dogs, are better than all other life forms. We talked about her show career, and she believed she was the best princess ever. Other breeds of dogs? They were just dogs. They were okay to look at but not that interesting.

In Gig Harbor, Pepper determined that she was no longer required to spend the day in the covered run with the dogs. After all, she was the Head Princess. You might ask, *how did Pepper let you know?*

Pepper lay on the couch, immobile, not even five Clydesdales could have pulled her off the couch. There was no discussion, and there was no force that could compel her into the run.

"Pepper decided the children could go down to the dog run. I'm not going down there anymore. Uncle Phinney can take care of them," Sally said. "Upon our return from work, Pepper would trot down to the run with us in order to liberate Molly, Trixie, Phinney, and Splash. She would stand next to the gate and bark instructions to her subordinates as the gate swung open. Pepper would then turn to trot back to the house with Molly on one side and Trixie on the other side. They would both nip at her ears as Splash and Phinney trailed behind."

From that day forward, no matter where we lived, she was simply and undeniably a house princess.

I think I misheard you. I thought I heard you tell me no. Occasionally, Sally would tell Pepper she couldn't do something such as go run errands in the car or accompany me to work. Pepper simply turned and walked away down the hall with her tail wagging. Upon Sally's return, she would be greeted by torn-up magazines or newspapers and a smiling, tail-wagging senior Bernese Mountain dog. Sally often said Pepper treated her like kitchen help. Pepper would respond, "And your point is what?"

She simply didn't believe in no. In Pepper's mind, "no" was for little people. This got her in trouble on more than one occasion when she went to Turtle Bay, in place of her well-behaved, little sister Molly who truly never did anything wrong her entire life. Pepper described Molly as "talented but unimaginative."

Her biggest day of trouble involved two offenses within minutes. It was just before an after-hours art opening. After-hours events include brownies or cookies, coffee, and punch. Everyone knew that. Everyone, including Pepper! We walked downstairs to where staff and Board members were gathering prior to the event. Pepper, of course, was not on a leash. In a blink of an eye, she disappeared into the restaurant kitchen where the goodies were on the counter. No one saw her. Ninjas would be envious of her cunning.

Moments later, the restaurant manager came back into the museum with Pepper in tow by the collar. Pepper wagged her tail. The restaurant manager, a self-proclaimed Curator of Fun, normally in good humor, was not smiling. Pepper had discovered the kitchen was unattended! According to Pepper's account, she asked, "Is anyone going to eat this?" Hearing no answer, she devoured a twenty-four-by-twenty-four-inch pan of chocolate brownies. Did she get sick? Of course not.

She wasn't finished with the day's antics. The Board Chair, a frumpy, sensitive, and standoffish person, entered the room. Pepper loved him. The feeling was not mutual. Pepper leaped into the air, placing her front feet on his chest as she wagged her tail. He nearly fainted or at least had to change his underwear.

Judy Salter, our CEO at the time, who Pepper and I loved dearly, shouted, "Son of a bitch!" This was a mild exclamation by Judy. She later left the museum to teach creative profanity to Navy Chiefs and Marines. No, she didn't, but she could have.

Following a period during which Pepper was banned from the museum, she returned coincidentally to the hiring of the fourth CEO in less than four years. It was a tough place to work. It was the CEO's first day at work. He occupied what had formerly been my office. I relocated to share an office with another vice president.

Unfortunately, the mechanism to hold his office door never really worked right. This caused me no trouble because I worked with an open door unless someone other than me was going to be crying, then the door was closed. We were having a lunchtime management team meeting in our conference room. Pepper saw the new CEO, and he was a guy! She simply had to meet him so that he could understand how blessed he was to have her as a staff member. But each time she slid between him and the staff member sitting next to her, he pushed her away.

After a few minutes of rejection, Pepper disappeared from the room. At the conclusion of the meeting, I left the room and was met by three of the staff members who looked grief-stricken! What happened? Pepper had left the meeting, pushed the door open to my old office, and ate the new CEO's lunch! The women were beside themselves. They loved Pepper, and she was on probation. One ran down the stairs to the restaurant and brought back an identical lunch. It was placed in his office, and the door was closed. He never knew.

Alas, one of the Board members complained about the dogs being at work and they were banished. Maybe it was because Pepper had been fired five times... If you asked Pepper, she would tell you she simply had too much to do at home and chose to go in a different direction. The day before my last day, the CEO told me to bring Molly and Pepper back to work so that the staff could say goodbye. It was a kind gesture from a man who never knew that Pepper ate his lunch.

Look for the easy mark, it's probably a man. Pepper loved men and was always gravitating toward them. It seemed to me that this was because she knew that we were more susceptible to her feminine wiles. Mom might say no to something she wanted to do, but Dad would always say yes. A long driveway led from the house to the manually operated gate.

On more than one occasion Sally said, "Pepper can't go to work with you today. She will just get herself in trouble." Sally would make Pepper sit and stay as I drove down the driveway. Arriving at the gate, I opened the gate. There was joyful Pepper jumping into the car to go to work. She had broken from her stay and ran full speed to the gate. It was time to go to work.

You're not going to eat that, are you? By now, you probably realize that Pepper recognized no authority greater than herself. She was a counter surfer and a trash can dumper without limits. Her little sister, Molly, was an angel who spent every day at Turtle Bay without incident. Molly and I frequently participated in meetings at Trilogy, the local architectural firm with architects James Theimer and Todd McEfee previously mentioned as a skirmish site for Molly and Annie Salter. Molly was well-behaved and always welcome. Scheduled meetings were at eight in the morning or earlier.

However, if Pepper was to participate in a morning meeting, a warning was required by Trilogy the day before. Why? No such warning was issued on two occasions. On both occasions, an unwary staff member opened Trilogy's front door, and a black, brown, and white blur of fur named Pepper flashed by. She raced through the office, snatched everyone's breakfast off their desks, and stopped to knock over the kitchen trash to uncover any food item hidden below the trash. At this point, she returned to the conference room for the meeting. Pepper claimed that she always asked, "Are you going to eat that?"

I love ice cream, but for a time I decided I would be thinner and enjoyed juice bars before bed. Each night, as I ate my juice bars, Pepper jumped onto the bed, placed her front feet on my chest, and took the juice bar right off the stick!

Sally would ask, "Why did you give her the juice bar?"

My response was, "She just took it."

Molly learned the same trick. Soon, they were eating half my juice bars.

Nobody says that to my little sister. Pepper was not a big dog, but as good old Mark Twain said, "It's not the size of the dog in the fight, but the size of the fight in the dog."

Although it had not held true for Phinney, it held true for Pepper. Many larger dogs ran at Pepper with their ears back. They would also growl at her. She didn't always bring out the best in dogs. Pepper either stood her ground, unflinching, or turned and walked away. No one ever attacked her.

However, on a spring afternoon in the Harbor, Molly and Pepper walked in front of me, leashed in tandem. A larger golden retriever named Brando approached from the opposite direction. We had seen Brando many times, and there was never any aggression. Molly, shorter than her older sister, was on the side Brando would pass. As Brando passed just behind Molly's head, he snapped at Molly's left flank. Faster than I could recognize anything had happened, Pepper, on a short leash, jumped over Molly's back and had the larger Brando on his back. Orange fur was flying. Pepper didn't show a spot of dog slobber on her back! I think Pepper heard Led Zeppelin's "Immigrant Song" in her head. We passed by Brando many times thereafter. His owner always gave me a dirty look. Molly and Pepper always looked over their shoulder at him and said, in singsong unison, "Hi, Brando!" Brando was speechless.

Live large until your last breath. Beads of seawater rocketed from Pepper's black and brown fuzzy legs that ended in white socks as she flew, not ran, down the beach. She splashed through the six-inch deep remains of the wave as it slickly flowed off the sand into the green, foamy Coronado surf. *Whoosh* went the three-foot-high waves as they crashed on the gently sloping beach.

Point Loma loomed behind the long, flat beach. Coronado's dog beach, known to us as South Princess Beach, was just south of North Island Naval Air Station. A wisp of an offshore breeze gently fluffed Pepper's gorgeous Bernese Mountain dog suit as she raced parallel to the shore. Her back was straight, and her tail stuck out behind and wagging. The skirt on her back legs blew in the breeze and her eyes were wide open, filled with a brilliant light rarely seen in the eyes of any being. Her ears were pulled back by her momentum, and her pink tongue lolled forward to the left side of her open mouth as if she were laughing with joy. A greyhound at the track couldn't cover the distance between us any faster than Lady P burned down the beach.

She pulled up short with a splash, standing in her inimitable self-confident, stiff-legged I-am-way-too-damn-cool-for-words stance. Her front legs were firmly set in the sand beneath the shallow water and her tail was wagging wildly from side to side as she shouted a sharp, gleeful, "Woof!" micrometers from the face of her younger, stouter best friend in the whole wide world, baby sister and greatest admirer, Molly Marie. It was as if to say, "Why are you standing there? Don't you get it? We're at the beach! Time to run! Time to play!"

Molly didn't flinch but her head snapped toward Pepper and her face seemed to say, "What? Don't you realize Mom has cookies?"

Molly never met a cookie she didn't like. That's not fair. Molly never met a food item that she didn't like. Molly's idea of a good day at the beach was to be glued to Mom's side like a fuzz ball remora, getting the arms and legs of her suit wet only absolutely necessitated by the location of the cookie pouch around Sally's slender waist. It was suspended eighteen inches above the surface of the wave's backwash because Mom was wading.

Molly's drooling made Pavlov's dog feel like an amateur! His research would have ended on day one if Molly had been one of his subjects. Pepper's joy of life, Molly's inadvertent clown-like, always the straight man antics, the bright blue sky, and Sally's laughter that leaped up from her very core because of the antics of her oldest fur children slapped a smile on my face. There was no better day at the beach than a day with my three senior girls, the girls whose love gave me peace. There has not been and will never be a better day in life.

Pepper loved running the Sacramento River Trail. Along the way, there was a creek to wade in. Occasionally, deer smells, mountain lion smells, squirrels, jackrabbits, cats, and even a snake would be on the path. The most fun of all? Deer to chase! Sally might gamely hang on to three of the girls, but not to Pepper. Off she would go with zero chance of catching her desired prey.

"Highlights of Pepper's Sacramento River Trail walk were splashing in the creek when the walk was nearly over, or, if I wasn't paying attention, taking off after a deer or a cat," Sally said.

But that wasn't the very best part of the River Trail… That was Grandpa Biscuit. Grandpa Biscuit was a WWII veteran in his eighties but not that kind of veteran. He was a German motorcycle soldier, delivering messages through enemy lines. He was twice apprehended by Allied forces during the war and escaped the first time!

Pepper and Molly spotted him from at least one hundred yards away, and they knew he carried dog biscuits! No force could hold them! They stripped the leash from our hands and ran full stride toward this slender, elderly gentleman who was walking with sticks. Other walkers who did not know the girls or Grandpa Biscuit looked on with horror. They seemed to think, "Oh, no, that poor old man is going to be devoured or at least crippled by Bernese Mountain dogs. What can we do?"

He was not devoured or crippled. He loved the girls. Pulling up short, they sat at his feet, gently taking the biscuits from his hand. He was a kind soul. I miss him and all the people and animals that have passed briefly along my path in life.

If you aren't getting dirty, you aren't having fun. Up and down Pepper would race in her seasonal creek, splashing mud and water over her suit. The creek ran for at least fifty yards and Pepper joyously ran its length for hours. The poor tadpoles that lived in the creek were subjected to Pepperian selection. They must have seen their entire tadpole lives flashing before their eyes. No matter where we lived, at bath time, Pepper would be the dirtiest. Dirt ran off her fur like a muddy stream.

Anyone can steer the Enterprise when the Klingons are not around. My fingers gently probed Pepper's abdomen as she stood calmly beneath me. How many animal bellies had my fingers sought to find any subtle abnormality over these last twenty-five years that I practiced veterinary medicine? Ten thousand? Twenty thousand? More? Less? Who knew and did it matter right now? Dogs, cats, monkeys, wolves, leopards, baboons, you name it. If it had fur or feathers, my fingers would seek the secrets contained in the size, consistency, and position of the organs contained in their bellies.

How many times had these fingers rubbed the soft, white fleece on Pepper's belly? It was always neatly parted in the middle as she lay next to me wagging her tail and smiling. Just yesterday, I did so, admiring what a beautiful girl she was and had always been. Pepper always oozes class, even in a mud-splattered suit that followed a run through the seasonal creek in front of our Redding house.

What a priss! Pepper's tail wagged side to side as she softly panted. Her mind told me, "I trust you, Dad. But you know you are looking in the wrong place. You know, you have known in the back of your mind for a very long time what will take me away. You are and have been scared to be right because you can't write a different ending!"

What a self-confident, smarty pants she was! She always saw right through me. All my girls always have seen right through me.

I thought her belly was not taut. She wasn't tense and her belly was not painful. Yes, both kidneys were where they were supposed to be, the left one a bit farther back, high up under the lumbar vertebrae, and, yes, they were smooth and seemed to be the right size. All the loops of her gut felt fine, I didn't feel any obstructions, although I didn't think I would since her morning poop at the beach six hours earlier, picked up and bagged immediately, was normal as normal can be.

How about her spleen? She was pale and panting. It could be from loss of blood. Did she have the dreaded and highly aggressive tumor of the spleen, hemangiosarcoma? That wouldn't be so bad because, if detected early, a splenectomy and some good drugs (such as epoetin to stimulate her bone marrow to rapidly produce oxygen-carrying erythrocytes) could buy her, really us, more time. No, her spleen was right where it should be. It was lying against the left side of her stomach, smooth and normal in size, just as I knew it would be. How about her liver? No reason to think that she had liver disease since she had no clinical signs of liver disease. Her liver was right where it should be and felt just like it should feel.

Let me feel her chest. I placed my hands on both sides of her chest, along her sides, just like I have done countless times before. I stroked the soft, long, black silky fur and told her, "I love you, girl. I don't know if I can get by without you. You are one of the brightest lights, the greatest loves of my life."

I felt her heart pounding, but her chest was not expanding and contracting with each breath. She was breathing with her entire abdomen! Fear filled me as I thought, *I think she has fluid in her chest and my guess is it's from neoplasia.* My worst fears were coming to pass. I felt helpless, unable to influence what was to come in a positive direction.

Pepper looked up and toward me, wagged her tail, and seemed to say, "You know better, Dad. You know I must go. My time is ending, and I can't do more. I'm not sad. I know you are, but I couldn't have enjoyed a happier life. Nobody ever has! I have never even had a bad day! I've pretty much done it all. I've raised kids and kicked tails at dog shows while I quickly finished my championship which I enjoyed more than any girl should on the catwalk. I don't even know why those other girls showed up. They would have been better off investing their entry fees in pig ears. I have had the best parents and brothers in the world, the best friends, lived in Oregon, Washington, California, gone on vacations, ran on the beach, eaten hundreds of ice cream cones at Dairy Queen, hundreds of hamburgers, plain or plain with cheese, of course, at In and Out and who didn't love me? Who didn't I bring joy to? Well, those few folks, they just didn't matter because they were, well, basically, they were just stupid. It was their loss. Why, I even had jobs! I worked in a museum, helped at Board meetings, helped build an arboretum, helped open exhibits, greeted visitors, and loved small children and every puppy I have ever seen. You remember how scared Dr. Robyn was when I walked through the glass exhibit at Turtle Bay Exploration Park before it opened? The devil himself wouldn't have scared her more! But being the lady that I am, I didn't even graze a molecule of the exhibit. I have walked thousands of miles, up hills and down, along harbors, bays, by the Sacramento River with you, Mom, my baby sister, my daughters, and the Schnauzer. And I have never gotten old! I don't have a single gray hair. I am the oldest puppy that has ever lived! Could it have been better? No! Absolutely not! On top of that, I have had Molly, my best friend and the best baby sister. She's the funniest, most serious, little clown that a girl could ever have to bring me joy and share my joy. No, it couldn't have been better, and you know what they say, 'the brighter the flame, the faster the candle burns,' and I have burned a brilliant, brilliant white — well, black and brown and white. You'll get through it. I will always be with you with my fuzzy little bottom and wagging tail in front of you. Remember me in my royal purple necklace or collar, as you might say, on the end of my royal purple leash in tandem with Molly, in every memory of every walk we ever did and there, yes, there by you, on every walk you'll ever take for the rest of your life. Don't worry. I'm okay. We will be together again soon. You must stay; your work isn't done. Daddy, you aren't, and probably never will be, as smart as I am. But as Trixie Lou would say, you are a boy and boys are, not that I agree with her, completely stupid!"

Tears streamed down my face as the cool ocean breeze passed over us from San Diego Bay as we lay next to each other on the prickly, dried short grass in Nonie's backyard. However, there weren't any tears for Pepper. She was way smarter, way kinder, and way better than I would ever be. No, the tears were for me, for Sally, and for everyone who Pepper ever touched and allowed, I do mean allowed, to be a part of her life and to share in her joy and light. I knew she was right, but I wouldn't, couldn't, accept that my time with Peppermander was rushing to an end like an out-of-control locomotive.

"I know, sweetheart," I said., "But I am not ready for you to go. This is way too hard."

Way too hard for me, a guy who has witnessed hundreds of animal deaths over the years. Way too hard for a guy who had performed thousands of necropsies on animals in attempts to learn why they had died and how I could have made their lives better and saved them. Way too hard for somebody who spent the last week of his dad's, Bompsie's, life with him in a hospital. Way too hard for me.

She lifted her head and turned slightly toward me. She was still panting but was wagging her tail as I talked. In my mind, I heard something she had told me many times over the years. "Well, Daddy, you remember what I have always told you. Anybody can steer the Enterprise when the Klingons aren't around. You know that I, Peppermander, unlike you, Daddy, can steer the Enterprise when the Klingons or the Viking Kittens are around. In fact, if I steered the Enterprise, the Klingons would better head for home with their tails between their legs, if they had tails. You'll be alright; I will never leave your thoughts, your dreams, your memories, or your side. Little P will always be right beside you, next to Phinney, Splash, Lori, Abigail, [and] all the fur children that have tried to guide you through life. I'll always be your little girl, and you'll always be my dad!"

It was a tough, way past tough, afternoon and evening. We needed to get home. We needed to give Pepper something to make her more comfortable. Over the last three hours, her panting had become more frequent, and her color was paler. She stayed outside in the backyard, sitting up on the grass with her nose a couple of inches higher than it should be. She didn't come into the house to beg at dinner with the other girls.

"Pepper really has me vexed. I don't like her breathing at all," I said.

"We need to get her home where you can give her some analgesics. Do you think that we need to do anything else for her?" Sally replied.

I answered no as the reality, the seriousness and finality of her illness knocked down every door of self-defense and denial my mind could construct. "She seems well hydrated. I don't think that there is anything else that is going to help her right now."

It was cool and dark when we got home, but Pepper leaped out of the Mandermobile like the ageless puppy that she was and ran into the house barking and shouting with all the other girls. How could I accept that she was terminally sick? During the day she walked four miles, coughing a bit. She had been to her favorite Coronado Dog Beach, waded in the water, visited Nonie's house, and picked up Sally at the end of her shift at the San Diego Zoo. The Chili Babies, Pepper's daughters, Abigail Vaughn Mander and Mandy Marie Mander, immediately got into one of their sisterly scuffles that often accompanied excitement. It was soon followed by their apparent name-calling and who said what and when.

Sasha jumped in, also pounding on the smaller Mandy.

"No!" I shouted at them. "Knock it off."

Sasha looked up at me and seemed to say, "Vat? You know I am a ferocious Giant Schnauzer. I live for this kind of thing. Ve must have order!"

Yes, I know, I thought. *But I am just not up for this tonight.*

We subcutaneously injected Pepper between her shoulders with a small amount of butorphanol, a narcotic analgesic that could make her breathe more comfortably. We hoped that she would rest comfortably through the night. We were exhausted, beyond exhausted, emotionally more than physically and Sally had to be up at o'dark thirty to get ready to drive to the Zoo. We would look at Little P in the morning and figure out what to do next.

* * *

"Sally, have you seen Peppermander?" I asked as she scooped less than a cup of tan pelted kibbles into five of six clay-colored bowls that sat high on a tattered cream-colored Formica-topped kitchen island.

It was four o'clock in the morning. Sally stood at the island in her red flannel nightie which pictured giant pandas holding assorted poses or chewing on short bamboo sticks. Sally's hair was growing. It was down her neck in back, and she looked tired from worry and lack of sleep, just like I felt this morning, if you can call the predawn hours morning. Panda eyes, that's what I thought Sally had this morning. I hated to think what I looked like.

Every morning began this early at our house. We'd be awakened by a jolting combination of the alarm clock going off and Bernese Mountain dogs and a Giant Schnauzer jumping on and off the bed. They'd stomped on appendages, internal organs, and any body parts of ours that their fuzzy feet could rest upon. It would be accompanied by a repetitive, deep, loud breakfast song sung verse by identical verse by our second oldest fur child, Molly Marie. Believe me, Molly's incessant breakfast song was no more welcome or melodic after hearing it for six years than it was the day she launched her singing career in our Gig Harbor home.

"No, she hasn't come in yet. I haven't seen her," Sally replied.

Our almost nine years with Pepper had passed in the blink of an eye. Pepper missed a meal here or there over the last three weeks. We tried tempting her with a variety of culinary treats ranging from cheese, chicken breast, eggs, gravy, various kibble, pasta, and anything else we might have in the refrigerator. Finally, we offered the nasty canned dog food that served as her sole acceptable fare, eaten in her whelping box from a spoon, when she was raising her first two Berner fur balls, Bailey, and Trixie.

At first, the variation in diet worked and, after a thorough inspection, Pepper slowly ate the offering after waiting until the other five girls gulped down their food like piranhas just coming off the South Beach diet. When they were done, they watched her analyze her meal through the oak slats of the baby gate which separated her from the ravenous horde. Pepper made her decision. Would she eat the food on her own? Would she eat it if Sally fed it to her off a spoon? Would she walk away, lie down, and wait for the youngsters to descend upon it like a pack of push-pig hyenas? After a few days, even a variety failed. She had eaten about five bites of people food in the previous 24 hours.

"Where is your headlamp?" I asked with fatigue in my voice.

I hadn't slept well the night before. I was filled with fear that Pepper's health challenge was more serious than the arthritis in her right knee that developed because of a torn anterior cruciate ligament or the mild dental disease that Sally and I found the day before during a physical examination. Being a veterinarian and being a career animal trainer and keeper like my lovely wife, Sally, doesn't make it easier to be parents to fur children. My heart tells me it makes it harder, just like I imagine it is harder for a pediatrician to care for their own children because you know how they can become ill, know how they can suffer, and are way too familiar with the consequences of disease, decline, and the quickness with which a life force can depart this plane. You are painfully aware of the fragility of life, having seen generations of animals pass on that were under your personal care or the care of your colleagues.

We lived in a state of denial from the time Pepper first coughed several months prior. It was a dry, harsh cough, echoing from deep within her chest. The cough came first thing in the morning, ran through a few quick coughs, and was over for the day. Sometimes halfway through her now occasional four or five-mile walks, Pepper coughed for a few minutes. After that, the cough was gone for the day. Since she had a great appetite, a great enthusiasm for life, and the auscultation of her chest was unremarkable, it was easy to ignore these first, early warnings. However, we never succeeded in pushing it out of our minds. We were all too aware of abbreviated, fiercely joyful lives lived by many Bernese Mountain dogs. We knew their too-bright candles could be burned out by various kinds of neoplasia such as histiocytoma.

Why did we ignore it? How could we ignore it? We didn't want to believe our little girl wouldn't be with us, to give us joy, until she was old and gray. A local, very talented veterinarian who confirmed radiographically that she had some chronic arthritic changes in her right knee also failed to hear anything unusual in her chest a couple of months before. He gave us great relief when he ruled out the possibility that her sore leg was due to the ravage of osteosarcoma, one of the most aggressive and least treatable neoplasia any lifeform can fall victim to. Also, to our relief, her cough had stopped a few weeks ago. *We missed a bullet*, we independently told ourselves.

I called Pepper as I walked what suddenly seemed a long way down the parquet-floored hall to our bedroom. "Pepper, Peppermander," I called as I walked. However, the joyful head princess didn't appear in front of me as I neared the open sliding glass door that led to the deck adjacent to our bedroom and the girls' grass-covered backyard.

Ever since San Diego's version of winter had ended just after the first of the year, we had removed the "doggie door" and left the sliding glass door open so the girls could come and go as they pleased throughout the night. The inexpensive price tag for their comfort was endless vacuuming opportunities and a bedspread and sheets that perpetually felt like you were camping in the desert or sleeping at the beach. Was Pepper even worse off than I feared the night before? Did she pass on quietly on her beloved cool grass with the breeze in her hair while we tried to sleep just a few yards beyond with her sisters and daughters?

I put Sally's headlamp on and stepped off the deck and onto the damp grass. It was very dark and a little foggy as my eyes scanned the yard. No, the headlight's beam reflected in her tapetum lucidum, the reflective covering the back of dog and cat eyes that gathers light and provides them night vision superior to ours. She was on her feet! As I called to her from the center of the grass, she slowly made her way up the grassy hill, wagging her beautiful furry tail as she approached.

We walked together up the hill, up the steps of the deck, and into the bedroom. In the light of the bedroom, I could see she was covered with dew since she had slept outside all night. She was also panting with greater force and frequency than the night before. As Sally and I dried her with a towel, she stood wagging her tail. She was panting hard, much too hard for a girl that had slept outside in the cool night air and was covered with dew. A knot grew larger and larger in the pit of my stomach as I examined the mucous membranes of her mouth. They were pale and slightly muddied, much worse than the evening before. The knot grew larger until I felt my belly might burst as I tried to examine her chest for airway sounds. The sounds that I had heard with welcome the morning before were gone. I could only hear the pounding of her heart and it was reflected throughout her being.

Reality swooped into our room like a grim wall of rain. Pepper would not light our lives for years, months, or even days. Her time was over. Best case? Congestive heart failure. What a condition to hope for, right? It was often treatable, and life could be extended. The quality of life could improve through proper drug therapy. However, many signs of congestive heart failure were not present. There had not been an insidious onset and no damp airway sounds. Instead, the disease had come upon Pepper with lightning speed. The most likely case? Thoracic neoplasia. It was untreatable. It was uniformly and rapidly fatal from the time of detection in an animal like Pepper.

Sally continued to get ready for work as we talked about which emergency veterinary service Pepper and I would visit. Sally knew it was grim, but she was brave. That's how honey badgers are. Sally had cared for, comforted, raised, and trained all kinds of domestic and wild animals for over three decades. She knew that Pepper needed help and needed it now. We needed radiography, blood analyses, and the critical care expertise possessed today by emergency veterinary specialists.

Sure, I had practiced emergency medicine on monkeys, sea lions, antelope, wolves, gorillas, dolphins, and even killer whales for over two decades, but I didn't have the in-depth expertise or resources of today's emergency practitioners, their highly trained support staff, or their equipment. We discussed the merits of a couple of facilities within a half-hour drive. Sally reminded me that she had an excellent experience a few months before when Pepper, waiting until I was out of town as she usually did for her health challenges, had an acute abdominal crisis. She was right. Pepper and I would travel to the local facility located a mile away.

Attaching Pepper's royal purple leash to her royal purple collar, befitting the unquestioned head princess that she had always been, she and I walked up the small incline to Pepper's PT Cruiser. It was white with purple and silver flames. I opened the back door and Pepper stopped at the door. She was very willing to go with Dad, just like always, no matter how near, how far, or what the destination was. However, she didn't feel well enough to jump in on her own. I gently lifted her and placed her on the back seat, fearing that it might be our last ride together.

Up the driveway, down our little lane, and around the corner, Pepper and I drove. I could hear her panting in the back seat. As we negotiated the twists and turns on the narrow road, my mind was filled with more fog than what covered the landscape around us. Sally had made sure that I knew the way to the clinic. It was necessary to make sure because I often have memory lapses when tired. Well, really, I often have memory lapses, period. Arriving at the brightly lit clinic, I opened the back door of the car and Pepper jumped out with an agility that argued against her discomfort.

She wagged her tail as we walked up the steps to the clinic.

"Pepper was always happy. It didn't matter where she was or what was going on," Sally said.

Unlike some fur children, Pepper welcomed her rare visits to veterinary hospitals. Maybe she was used to the sights and smells from home? More likely, she had always been treated with kindness and respect by veterinarians and their assistants — first by Dr. Bob and Dr. Jan at the Purdy Veterinary Clinic in western Washington where she was weighed on a regular basis and where she and Sally took Bailey and Trixie for their check up the day after they were born. Later, she was treated with equal love by Dr. Gary and his staff at the Redding Animal Hospital in northern California. Most recently, she had been treated with kindness by Dr. George Shinzakie at his Poway, California practice.

Tony, one of the clinic's animal health technicians, met us at the door. I identified myself as a veterinarian and scrolled through Pepper's complete medical history which was amazingly brief. As I held Pepper up gently with my arm under her chest, Tony listened to her chest and took her temperature, something Pepper always had regarded as beneath her dignity. Tony informed me that Dr. Tedder would see Pepper in just a moment. Pepper and I lay upon the cool, linoleum-covered floor, she on her chest and me on my side looking into her eyes. As I stroked her silky fur, she panted, wagging her tail as I told her how much I loved her and how sorry I was that she felt so bad.

Dr. Tedder entered the room in her white lab coat over her surgical green scrubs. I noticed one of her patients had run a muddy foot over the front of her left pant leg. She was smiling with a stethoscope around her neck. We introduced ourselves, and I spun through Pepper's complete medical history, giving the most detail concerning the last few days.

I told her what I couldn't state to Sally at home. "Dr. Tedder, I fear that Pepper has a pleural effusion, a chest full of fluid, probably due to advanced thoracic cancer."

Dr. Tedder kneeled quietly next to Pepper, gently placing her stethoscope against Pepper's chest, and listened for a minute.

She stood and said, "You may be right. I can't hear any airway sounds. We need to get Pepper on some oxygen to make her more comfortable and take some chest radiographs. Tony will bring the gurney so that we can roll her into the back. We don't want her to be uncomfortable."

Emergency veterinarians and their technicians are angels without wings. Dr. Tedder was no exception.

Tony and Dr. Tedder gently lifted Pepper onto the gurney and rolled her back into radiology. Pepper went wagging her tail.

I said, "I'll wait out here," knowing that it is often easier on pets and veterinary personnel if the owners stay out of the way during procedures. I called Sally to fill her in.

"Hello," she answered. I could hear the fear, sadness, and fatigue in her voice. She hadn't gone to work.

"Hi, sweetie. Pepper is in the back on some oxygen. Dr. Tedder is taking some thoracic radiographs."

"I can't go to work. I need to come to the clinic. I'll call and let them know that I just won't be of any value today," Sally said.

"You're right, doll. Come over as soon as you can."

A few eternal minutes later, the door to the exam room swung open and Dr. Tedder walked through the doorway with a profound look of sadness on her face.

"I am very sorry. You need to come and look at the radiographs with me," she said.

We walked past Pepper lying on her chest on the gurney. Tony briefly removed the oxygen mask, and I could see that the mucous membranes of her mouth were pinker which meant she was more comfortable. Her red blood cells had been recharged with oxygen, making it easier for her to breathe now. Pepper looked at me, and I patted her head as I walked by. She wagged her tail and said, "I'm fine. What's the big deal?"

Dr. Tedder and I stood around the corner looking at a pair of Pepper's chest films. It is always a difficult moment for a veterinarian when radiographs reflect an untreatable illness. In most cases, the veterinarian has the grievous task of explaining to the client the condition of their beloved pet, the cause of their illness, and options for treatment. Most of the time, the attending veterinarian has a few minutes to weave this story for the client. Not this time. My broken heart went out to Dr. Tedder at this moment because the instant that I looked at the films with her, she was aware that I knew my fears had been correct. In front of my eyes were radiographs of the most severe thoracic disease that I have seen in over twenty-five years of radiographs.

"I had hoped that we might see evidence of congestive heart failure," she said. "We can treat that but look here. You cannot even see the outline of the heart. Her chest is filled with fluid. Here's a large mass in front of where her heart should be. Another back here in the caudal ventral area of the lung. And…" She then pointed to a white opacity in Pepper's upper lung field. "[this] may be evidence of metastasis."

I felt the walls of the room instantly fade away. It seemed dimmer, and I knew that Pepper would not be going home with me. There was no option for her other than a gentle transition through euthanasia. Every moment without supplemental oxygen would be pure agony for Pepper.

"Her mom will be here shortly," I said with a voice that didn't sound like my own.

"I am so sorry," Dr. Tedder said as she gently took my arm and walked me back to the exam room. "We'll bring her back to spend as long as you want with her. Just knock on the door or come and get us when you are ready."

Crushed, I leaned against the exam room wall, waiting to see the headlights of Sally's van drive up. Tony brought Pepper back in and placed her on a soft orange and pink bath towel that had a border of tropical fishes around the edges. I don't even remember how she was taken off the gurney. Did I help? Did Tony do it all by himself? I didn't remember the day after it happened.

Pepper and I lay on the exam room floor until Sally arrived. Sally came in, put her arms around me, and we both sobbed.

"No, no, no, this isn't happening. I am not ready to lose her," she said.

I held Sally for minutes. I felt as if I was feeling as much pain as possible when I said, "She can't go home with us. I don't know how she has done as well as she has. No one should be able to run and jump and love life less than eight hours ago with a chest like Pepper's. I have never seen such severe thoracic disease."

Together, we lay on the floor with Pepper, thanking her for all she had given us over the years. The day that we had feared forever had come home to roost. Pepper needed to cross the Rainbow Bridge where she could recover and be pain-free.

"She needs to go home to be with Bompsie, Phinney, and Splash even though he moved out on us," Sally said.

Time stood still. Pepper's panting was the only sound. The room seemed to expand and the walls vanished. Sally got up to take care of some paperwork. Pepper stood and walked to the door, thinking it was time to go home.

"No, Pepper," I gently told her. "We can't go home. You have done all that you can do."

Pepper, still being Pepper, said, "Oh, bullshit. I am just fine."

Pepper cursed like a Marine Gunnery Sergeant to her very end. Where did she learn those words? Probably from her Grandpa Bompsie. We returned to the exam room, she lay on the floor, and we kneeled beside her.

I looked at my lovely, sad wife, with whom I had shared Pepper's entire joyful life with and said, "I will let them know that we are ready."

Sometimes knowing what is coming and knowing what needs to be done does not make it easier, it makes it harder. Pepper lay on her chest and Sally was in front of her, stroking her beautiful coat and talking to her. Kneeling next to her, I rubbed her under the chin, making sure that she didn't turn her head toward Dr. Tedder as she inserted the tiny, sharp butterfly catheter and expertly placed it within her cephalic vein.

Pepper didn't flinch. Bravery and trust were two of her strong suits. As Dr. Tedder quietly attached the syringe containing the euthanasia solution, I wanted to cry out, "No. Please don't," but I knew that it was right and fair for Pepper. She should suffer no more. There was a slight quiver of her lumbar muscles, and I felt her relax. Her head became heavy as she passed.

Dr. Tedder placed her stethoscope bell against her chest and confirmed what we all knew: Pepper was gone. Never again would we see her bounding down the hall, shouting in joy when we returned home. Never again would we see her stand in the middle of the yard as the younger girls ran around and played, yelling, "No running!" as she always did when they ran. Never again would she prank the other dogs around the patio table by staring out into the expanse of the yard and barking as if something was there. She did this to motivate them to run and bark which allowed her to get all the available attention.

Just like Pepper said, *"Anyone can steer the Enterprise when neither the Klingons nor the Viking Cats are around."* I have no doubt that I can steer the *Enterprise* when the Klingons are around. I have done harder things in tougher situations. Saying goodbye to Pepper was a very different matter. Pepper had left her mischievous mark on many people.

I sent the following message to her fans the morning of her passing, September 5, 2005. Did I mention she died on my birthday so that I could never forget her passing?

Pepper left us at 0615 this morning. She suddenly developed inappetence a few days ago and halfway through yesterday, began panting and looking uncomfortable. The night before her chest sounded fine. Pepper, Aunt Janet, and I went to the beach at Coronado, her favorite place in the whole world yesterday, with Trixie Lou and Pepper's nephew, Teddie Eddie. It was a beautiful day, but she walked very slowly around in the water, stopping to stand, instead of doing her usual jumping, running, and barking. Pepper went with me to pick up Sally at the Zoo after work, stopped at Balboa Park first for a walk, and ran some errands with us. By the end of the day, she needed help to get into the van. She even turned down an ice cream cone. At this point, Sasha said, "Better dig a hole." During the evening, Pepper began panting and it was difficult to hear any lung sounds.

Being a Berner that was almost nine, this was a scary situation because the most common cause of acute difficulty breathing at her age is histiocytoma (a form of cancer of the chest) accompanied by fluid in her chest. I didn't want to believe it but was pretty sure it was true. She was still wagging her tail as she visited Grandma's.

This morning at 0400, it was obvious that she had slept outside on the wet grass and was covered with dew. She was very damp, pale, and still panting. We went into the local emergency room and the excellent staff took radiographs. They were the most dramatic chest films I have ever seen. Multiple tumors were present in her chest. I can't imagine how she continued to have so much fun, play so much, and be so happy her last few weeks. There was no way to help her. She was very uncomfortable, still wagging her tail, but it was clear her work was done.

Sally and I sat with her for a long time, not wanting to say goodbye and not wanting to believe it. We weren't ready for her to leave. At 0615, just as the sun came up, Pepper was helped onto the other side with Bompsie, Phinney, and Splash. I talked with her about this yesterday afternoon and told her we weren't ready for her to go. She said she had done all she could, never had an unhappy day in her life, never been sad, never done a bad thing unless Sally was in trouble with her, lived large (as you all know that have been around her), and never got old. She said we'd be together soon, but for now, Molly was in charge and would try to keep me out of trouble with the assistance of Trixie Lou. She also said she didn't want her picture in the Berner magazine with the dead Berners, but I could send a note to some of the people that she loved and who loved her. You all helped her have a full life, and we hope she helped yours be fuller. Thank you for all you gave her.

Folks like Pepper spend all their time giving, loving, and having fun. They don't waste time not being nice so their candles burn very fast.

I know we will all miss her, and we all know that we have been very lucky to share her life.

Thanks for being generous with your time and love.

Pepper had lots of fans, and some of them sent notes back to me.

Paul and Karen Povey had adopted Trixie's sister, Bailey. She was one of the best dogs I have ever known.

"Oh my gosh, I am so surprised and saddened by your news. What a shock! I guess I thought that Pepper would always keep going. I suppose it was a blessing that she did so well right up to the end instead of facing a long decline. She was a wonderful soul and will be missed. Bailey wishes she could come sit on your feet right now to help you feel better. Brian, your letter was lovely and a wonderful tribute to a wonderful girl. I really loved the story about Belker – very well said. I hope you guys get some comfort from knowing she had the best life any Princess could have hoped for, and she spread her good spirit far and wide. We will miss her," Karen wrote.

James Theimer, the Redding architect whose staff sometimes lost their breakfasts to the marauding Pepper wrote, "I am sorry to hear about Pepper; she was a real sweetheart. Your story is certainly true: just this morning as I was reflecting on the stress-filled life that is mine, I thought of Barley as a constant comfort: much like the tribbles in that old Star Trek episode. All you need to do is pet them to be soothed." Barley was James's golden retriever, and he was a fine dog.

James's wife, Sunnie, sent a separate note. "James just informed me of your loss. How very sad. Some would say Pepper is just a dog. Not I. Nor James. Nor you. She is and will be forever a part of who you are, through your shared experiences, in your memories, and certainly in your heart. It is why I have decided to be a chicken and consciously chosen not to have another dog after Barley. It just gets too hard to say goodbye. Don't know if you believe this, but I believe that just like the human spirit/soul, our dogs will hook up with us again in another existence, maybe in another format, but we'll know each other, and that connection is enduring across space and time and the limitations we now know on this earth. Mourn her. Celebrate her. But always hold her close. My sincere condolences. Sunnie."

Judy Salter, the CEO of Turtle Town who allowed the girls to be part of the Turtle Town staff and yelled, "Son of a bitch!" when Pepper jumped up onto the Board chair, wrote, "What a wonderful dog. My life is so much better for having known her. What a princess of a dog with such a sense of joy and grace. Thank you for sharing this with me. Annie, however, is not as upset and just wants to know if she can bite Molly for old times' sake. Maybe that is just her way of grieving too."

Jacque Holden, Turtle Town's Human Resource Director wrote, "I read this at home last night and shed tears for you all. Miss Pepper was such the good girl. She had sneaky down to a science, a stomach that drove her to perfection, and love down to a pat. I will NEVER forget Miss Pepper with her excellent treat-sniffing nose, her ability to snatch treats out of the air, and her ability to barter for a pat with a close body snuggle and nose. I love that she had no qualms about filling her belly and looking at you with those bright, alert eyes that said you were so good to let her have whatever you gave her! She's certain to know that Mom, Dad, the girls, and the boys are all missing her greatly. I bet her sisters are wondering where she got to go and just when she's coming back. They just don't know that she's waiting to welcome them up to doggy heaven when their time comes too. Put your arms around one another and give each other a big hug. And know that all of us wish that we could be there hugging you too. The princess is gone. She will be missed. However, the end came fast for her, and she didn't have to suffer long. TO THE GREAT PEPPERMANDER. YOU WILL BE MISSED. She had great parents who will always remember her."

Dr. Annie Seefeldt, animal chiropractor and one of my closest friends, wrote, "What a beautiful girl. Ms. Pepper sure picked the right Mom and Dad for this time around. She must have been a REALLY good girl on her last visit to earn you guys this time. You made the right decision for her. She knew you would, that's why she decided you were the peeps for her way back when. I'm sure she'll be very busy for a while getting heaven in order and teaching Molly how to manage things, learning new ways to tell you what to do next from her new, limitless existence. I'm so sorry for your sadness. I know it well. It's part of the package that we choose when we decide to live with angels here on Earth. The little kids were right, they don't stay around long because they've already learned the ropes. I think that Ms. Etta, the Teeny Queen probably had lots of fun, welcoming Pepper to heaven. Etta even kind of looked like Pepper when they were both still in their earth suits, in a very miniature sort of way."

Chapter 23

UNCERTAINTY – THE WORLD AFTER PEPPERMANDER

Molly and Pepper were inseparable from the time Molly joined the family. Molly saw Pepper leave the house on her way to the emergency room and saw that she did not come back. For the next forty-eight hours, Molly lay sternal, immobile on the bedroom floor with her face between her paws. She was facing the doggie door, moving only to go outside to go potty, but not moving to eat her dinner. This happened for two days! Molly never missed meals, ever.

The other girls, Trixie, Mandy, and Abigail all came to see what she was up to over the course of those two days. They stood next to her, bending forward, touching her muzzle, and licking the side of her mouth. Maybe they were looking to her to become the head princess. They wondered why she would not move. We will never know. What Molly knew was her big sister and best friend was gone. Thereafter, Molly was hesitant to ride in the PT Cruiser, the car that took Pepper to the emergency room for her final ride.

There was uncertainty in the pack. Pepper had provided such strong leadership, been such strong support, and provided so much love. Who would step into her shoes or paws? Would it be Molly who had been respected and loved by Trixie, Mandy, Abigail, and Sasha? Or would it be Trixie? How would this be sorted and how long would it take?

That is a story for another day.

Chapter 24

LOOSE ENDS

You have seen how our dogs enriched many lives and wrapped their paws around many hearts. Likewise, our friends enriched the lives of our dogs. It is challenging for me to imagine the fifty-three years of my life I have shared without their presence; it would have been so bland. Has it been five decades? That sounds so long! I would not have received the love or learned lessons about love and life without them. They provided far greater joy and laughter than the sadness at their departure. This equation of emotion is strongly in my favor.

None of the dogs in this story politely or gently passed in their sleep. They all required gentle release to spare them further suffering, a process known as euthanasia, not to be confused with assisted suicide in humans, a contentious, but humane practice. Sparing animals from suffering, from my viewpoint, based upon a lifetime of animal experience, is an obligation. Many of my friends and colleagues see this responsibility extending from the animal's cradle to the grave.

They are not just animals. Some may take the biblical reference to "dominion over animals" to mean we can do anything we want to them. To me, this means we *always* have a responsibility to animals which includes providing a humane death to end their suffering. As was written in Proverbs 12:10, "A righteous man cares for the needs of his animals." It is not my fault that the Bible is sexist. However, the message is pure. How we treat our animals and the people with whom we share the Earth defines who we are.

Euthanasia decisions, even though they provide a gentle release from suffering, are very difficult. Decisions are complicated, personal, and emotionally charged. We never want to lose our pets; they are family, but it is our responsibility to consider the best interests of our pets. This means weighing how much our pets enrich our lives from the moment they join our family against our suffering when they depart. This decision carries with it an obligation not to let them suffer. In other words, we must temporarily set our loss aside and try to decide in their best interest.

Several considerations are included when trying to make the best decision concerning euthanasia. Prognosis, in other words, the likely course of the illness, is a primary consideration and requires gathering the most reliable information that is available. It is tempting to gather this information from online sources, but online sources are not always vetted and do not have the clinical information concerning an individual animal available to a veterinarian or veterinary specialist.

Medicine is an art, not a science, and defined answers as to how much time remains for the animal are not usually available. Clinicians rely on their experience, expertise, the animal's age, breed-specific information, treatment history, and clinical studies to make their best guess, which is usually a range. It is just a guess, the same is true for human life. A second consideration concerning treatment is the cost. Chemotherapy for animals and people is expensive. We are fortunate because, as a veterinarian, I can purchase drugs like Palladia directly from suppliers, but this option is not available for all owners. A third important part of the equation is the consideration of quality of life; this is possibly the most complicated consideration. There are online tools, print sources of information, and veterinarians who can aid with assessing the quality of life to help make euthanasia, but they all include similar questions to objectively make a very subjective decision. Gradual deterioration is sometimes harder to recognize than sudden deterioration in behavior. There are a few questions that I ask myself when considering euthanasia, including:

Can my pet perform all the normal behaviors they could once perform?

Are they affected by pain that can either not be alleviated or will alleviation result in them no longer enjoying life?

Are they eating, drinking, urinating, and defecating normally?

Do I think they are enjoying being here?

Marking good and bad days on a calendar can be a useful element of such decision-making, but the decisions are never easy, even for veterinarians. We all place the decision-making bar at a different location.

You have met several dogs during your reading, heard their stories, and, maybe, learned something about dogs or at least what my love for dogs means to me. Before we pop smoke, as we say in the military, I want to share experiences and thoughts concerning what it was like to have so many dogs at once. Not everyone is up for a pack.

As humans, we define and evaluate our lives by paradigm, including ethics and rationalizations. For many years, I believed that if any of us stepped into anyone else's thoughts, even if we loved them, we would ask, "Is that what you believe?" Because I believe this to be true, I have asked our extended family members who experienced the pack what it was like to share space with our dogs. By doing so, I hope to paint a more realistic picture to immerse you further in the joy that the dogs have provided for us all.

Our almost-daughter, Wendy, has frequently dog-sat for us over the last twelve years, and we have done the same for Wendy and Chris. I recently asked Wendy and Chris, "What was your first beach trip to Carlsbad with all the girls like for you and Chris?"

"Wendy and I had always had dogs, but not multiple dogs, just one dog at a time," Chris answered.

"I knew Sally walked all six of the dogs every day by herself: Trixie, Abigail, Mandy, Molly, Padi, and Sasha. Chris and I were used to the beaches in Oregon and Washington where you can take dogs to any beach. The girls loaded up into the van and were so excited. We could imagine them frolicking on the beach," Wendy recalled.

"We arrived by the beach in Carlsbad, got them out of the car, and they were pulling in every direction!" Chris exclaimed.

"The girls started toward the steep, cement stairs that led to the beach. I saw my life flash before my eyes because they were running down the steep stairs. I was having a hard time controlling them!" Wendy recalled.

"When we reached the bottom, an old man was reading us the riot act that no dogs were allowed on the beach. We hadn't seen the sign. We barely survived coming down the stairs. I tried to calm him down and explain and he went on and on. A crowd of spectators was gathering," Chris remembered.

"We trudged up the stairs and got all of them into the van, but Padi slipped out of her collar. She wasn't ready to leave! We were right by the busy coastal road and thought this would end in tragedy, but it didn't. We got into the van, panting heavily. At this point, we developed even more admiration for Sally and her ability to manage the girls," Sally noted.

Our almost-son, former Army Ranger Gabriel, stayed with us in Escondido while recovering from back surgery and between jobs. What happened when Sally and I returned from work?

"When both of you returned from a day of work, the pack became VERY loud and rambunctious. Pepper and Molly were at the head of the pack, ready to turn and snap a harsh instructional bark at one of her daughters who were crowding too close. Instruction and correction were Pepper's responsibility," Gabe said.

"Didn't you have a dog of your own while you stayed with us?" I asked Gabriel.

"At the time, my large Alaskan Malamute lived with us, a one-man dog, bigger than any of the other dogs in the pack. At first, I worried he would not fit into the pack. To Pepper's credit and his, she accepted him into her pack with open paws, yet to my astonishment, he followed her lead. I was concerned he might attempt to assert dominance, but he surrendered the decision-making process to Pepper. Pepper was a great lead dog," Gabe recalled.

Lieutenant Colonel Danny Skirvin, our very close friend, served in the United States Army Reserve Veterinary Corps with me. Danny lived in Phoenix during the time we lived in Escondido. Danny flew into San Diego International Airport every battle assembly weekend and stayed with Sally and me monthly for several years.

On Saturdays and Sundays, Danny and I drove to our Reserve Center, located almost ninety miles from home. We'd return to Escondido Saturday evening. On Sundays, I dropped Danny off at John Wayne International Airport for his return trip home. Because Danny looked like he was thirteen years old and in uniform, someone at the Airport always bought him dinner before he left.

I asked Danny, "What was it like when you came to stay with us in Escondido? "

"The first time I came to the house in Escondido, I thought, *that is a large volume of dogs*. There were dogs all over the place. I felt bad for Sasha because she was different from the others. I loved coming to Escondido to visit. It was a step away from reality. I enjoyed the cool fishpond in the backyard and the 37,000 pounds of dog. I had only met one or two Bernese Mountain dogs in my life. Your girls were the nicest damn dogs, always entertaining," Danny said.

"What was it like when we went to the beach or dinner with the girls? "I asked.

"Going anywhere was so much fun. All the girls piled in the back of the van, bounced around, and either leaned against you or sat on the bench next to you. Dogs surrounded you. I was anxious at first during the trips to Coronado Dog Beach or Fiesta Island. I hadn't spent a lot of time in dog parks and was concerned some evil dog might come out of nowhere and kill all the dogs. I do wish I could have seen more dog surfing. I worry the dogs developed a chronic tortilla chip deficiency since you left Escondido. The girls ate as many tortilla chips as we did at Cocina del Charro. You would tell them, no more chips, and someone would give them more," Danny recalled.

Hali Eden, another dearly loved member of our family, described what it was like to pet sit for the pack.

"I had never encountered so many big dogs in one pet-sitting session. I had never been around so many big dogs in one house. Abigail was the instigator. Entering the Escondido house, they would all gather in the entry, shouting. Abigail vied for dominance and would instigate a riot. It took some cookies to get everyone settled. Saylor and Sylvie came with me and there were eight dogs in the house. It was hilarious, fantastic dog energy. Everyone was doing their own thing, and everyone had their own interests. There was lots of fun and lots of dog energy. Thanksgiving, beach trips, and babysitting memories are all burned into my memory and heart. The trips to the Smokin' Bull Barbecue restaurant after a romp at Fiesta Island were great fun. The owner brought out giant, smoked bones for the girls. Of course, Della couldn't partake in Smokin' Bull because she became too growly at the other girls," Hali recalled.

We endure turmoil throughout our lives. Sometimes, it defines us. We often bring it upon ourselves, although we don't usually see it that way at the time. I was the poster boy for turmoil in my younger years. In my mid-thirties, I recognized dogs had always been my teachers. They accepted me no matter what I was like, made me better, and guided me through the morass of life. In my younger years, I didn't hear them. I ignored what they were trying to tell me. Over time, I listened and developed gratitude for dogs, their companionship, their wisdom, and their kindness.

We all have regrets in our lives. Sometimes, our regrets revolve around how we treated the people that we cared the most about. Sometimes, our regrets revolve around the decisions we made and the opportunities we let pass. Sometimes, they revolve around work or other performances. My biggest regrets? Not being as kind or appreciative of the dogs that tried to help me early in my life. They gave me unconditional love, and I was so confused that I didn't recognize theirs was the most generous, consistent force of positivity in my life.

Did the affected dogs suffer? I don't think so. In Tina, the English setter's case, the breeder insisted she go to a household that would invest more in her show career. It was a good home in Golden, Colorado. Arrow, the Gordon setter, went to a home with an Irish setter where they were loved and adored, but I let myself down by letting them move on. In time, I woke up and held the dogs I had known and loved dearly in my heart. I can always feel the souls of the departed surrounding me. They are much of the palette that colors the fabric of my life.

I recently asked Zachary, our son who is a talented companion animal veterinarian, to share his thoughts on how our family dogs affected his life. Before answering, Zack said, "The first veterinarian that I worked for in Idaho as a veterinary technician said I was too scattered and would never make it as a veterinarian. That probably motivated me to prove her wrong."

Zack continued, "I think it is important for kids to grow up with dogs. I grew up thinking it was super normal that we talked to our dogs like they were people. I mostly believed it when you said, 'Splash thinks you should go to your room.' Kids learn kindness, trust, and unconditional love. Tucker and Brodie, my golden retrievers, are always glad to see me, even though my wife is not. I remember making numerous jokes about dogs being more important than the kids. Dogs have helped me get through most of the sad times that are part of everyone's life. When you are at your worst or down, you can cuddle up to them and talk to them. They are nonjudgmental. You once told me that when you have two children or two dogs, more makes no difference. My wife, Cassie, was holding Harper, her liver and white springer spaniel in her Match. com photograph. That was one of the things that attracted me to her.

I am a veterinarian because of my childhood with dogs. I loved our dogs, loved other dogs, and wanted to be able to help them. I am impressed that dogs coming into the clinic are so trusting. They let us poke them and restrain them even though they don't know us, but they trust us to be kind. The relationship between families and companion animals has changed over the last few decades. They are treated like family members. Most companion animals now sleep inside the house on the furniture. [They are] no longer outside. However, we now see more anxiety disorders in companion animals."

The dogs, my fur children, I have written about touched many human hearts. Some, like mischievous Peppermander, will always be remembered for their antics. Some, like Phinneypin, Samantha, and Sasha, will be remembered for their devotion and loyalty. Some, like Pepper, Molly, and Trixie (all Bernese Mountain dogs) will live on through the many lives they touched.

If they are remembered, if anyone reads their stories, then they are still with us. Thank you for allowing me to share part of their stories with you. I hope you have enjoyed our time together. Dogs make us better, and they make life easier.

ABOUT THE AUTHOR

Dr. Joseph is from a small town near San Diego. He has a diverse career in animal and marine life care spanning five decades. He has worked across the U.S., Canada, and Asia in roles like animal keeper, veterinarian, and Executive Director.

Later, he joined the U.S. Army Reserve Veterinary Corps as its oldest veterinarian, retiring as a Major with numerous medals and awards.

He now provides veterinary consulting services for various North American aquariums, contributes through the American Humane Association, and trains veterinarians and farmers in developing countries through LifeStock International.

Dr. Joseph holds degrees in Zoology and Veterinary Medicine as well as a Master's in Fisheries and Aquatic Sciences. A prolific writer and speaker, he lives in Washington with his wife, dogs, and cat.

Made in the USA
Coppell, TX
03 September 2024

36752400R00121